SCARS

A Morbid Memoir

Eric Wiberg

Island Books

for VMJ-C

by the same author:

Bahamas in World War II
Mailboats of the Bahamas
U-Boats in the Bahamas
U-Boats off Bermuda
U-Boats in New England
Boston Harbor
Swan Sinks
Drifting to the Duchess (script & book)
Round the World in the Wrong Season
Tanker Disasters
Napoleon's Battles (co-author, Felix Wiberg)
Åke Wiberg (co-author, Mats Larsson)
Published Writing / Juvenilia
Yacht Voyages / Sea Stories
Travel Diaries

Published by Island Books, Boston, MA, USA

Copyright © 2020 Eric Troels Wiberg, ericwiberg.com

ISBNs 978-0-9998479-4-7, 0-9998479-4-5
E-book: 978-0-9998479-8-5, 0-9998479-8-8
Library of Congress Control Number: 2020915025

All rights reserved. No part of this publication may be reproduced in any manner without the prior written permission of the publisher, author, and photographer, except in the case of brief quotations embodied in articles or reviews.

For information, contact the author via eric@ericwiberg.com

Layout by Abdul Rehman Qureshi, writingpanacea@gmail.com

Printed in the United States of America

Table of Contents

Acknowledgements v
Foreword vii

Introduction 1
Part I: Shame Scars 12
Part II: Head 26
Part III: Hands & forearms 41
Part IV: Shoulders 54
Part V: Torso, front & back 59
Part VI: Legs, buttocks to feet 67
Part VII: Self-scarring 99
Part VIII: Surgeries 108
Conclusion 116
   Footnotes: *116*
   Cheeky Endnotes: *117*

About the Author 118

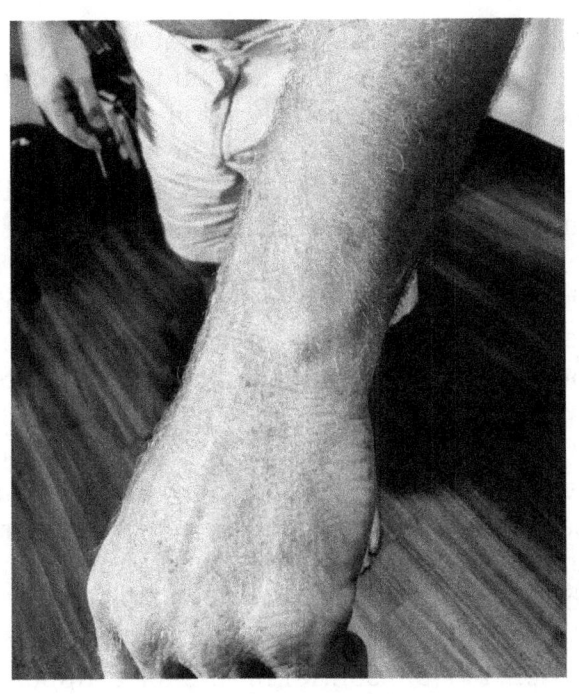

Acknowledgements

I thank the dermatologists who have treated me, in Newport, Nassau, Boston, Singapore, and New York, particularly the surgeons at Memorial Sloan-Kettering in Manhattan, the West Village, and Brooklyn, and Dr. Steven Kolenick at the Connecticut Dermatology Group, who after over decade without insurance performed a backlog of some dozen surgeries on my in 2006 and 2007, causing Yale

Medical School to send a small team to my office to photograph skin damage, take samples and interview me as a case-study of extensive skin damage.

I also am very grateful to licensed and trained photographer Caitlin D. Fitzgerald, also of the Boston area, for taking most of these photos in Newport with short notice. I thank my college friend R. T. W. for standing by me during some of the uglier episodes covered in this book, specifically the cigarette in kitchen, and right forearm before rugby practice. And M. C. who met me following several surgeries in New York City. My lifelong friend W. H. put some of this obsession with scars in perspective. Special thanks to our parents in Nassau, John & Sofia and James & Lynette in Nassau, and my sister Ann & Atle in Stockholm,

In the publishing world, I thank David Coffin, an inspiration, Bill Johnson, for his life-long support of my writing, Erin Niumata Cartwright at Folio in London for her support, as well as other publicists from home, Nicole Roberts at Bahamianology.com, and Kimberly King-Burns of the FB group ExpatsBahamas. I think friends new and long-time, including John R., Adrian W., Justin Z., Alexander R., George C., and Sten R. K., and Ed P.

As ever, I thank my editor Abdul Rehman Qureshi, the man behind the supply chain which is Island Books. As we approach the 20th book we collaborate on together, and I become happily and increasingly dependent on his skills and patience.

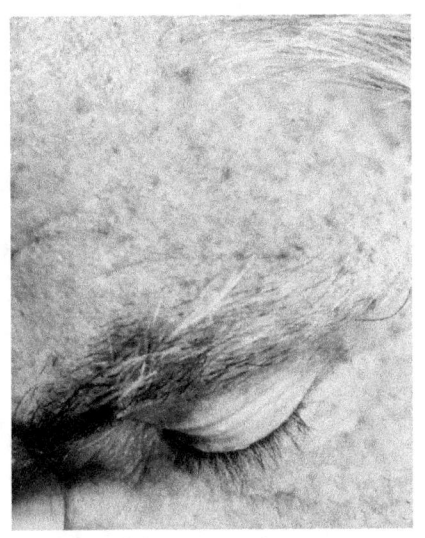

Foreword

A close friend from teenage years was thoughtful enough to share this recollection:

I remember you pointing out each scar you had way back when; I think 1987. I'm sure you have more now. You would tell me how you got each one; which reef, for example, or such. You would also tell me you thought having scars meant you were living life properly, and you thought you should get more.

I thought it was a bit misconceived, but fun non-the-less.

Introduction

The advertisement which I placed for a photographer for this book:

"I need a photographer, more artistic than just portraits, who can document some 30 physical scars - non nude - on my body, so that I can then write a short piece about each.

One is from a wrecked Japanese long-line fishing boat in the Kingdom of Tonga, another from a horse, burns, cuts, and so on. Not your typical photos of the family poodle, but not very avant-garde, either; I may need to get to the scar on a scalp, for example."

Responses: None.

Ultimate project photographer: Caitlin D. Fitzgerald, a private person and professional photographer.

This book began as a teen fantasy as I accumulated wounds from traveling four times round the planet, in over 80 nations or island groups. I travelled by land from Istanbul west to Perth, flying over the watery parts. I also voyaged by sea, in various stages from what was Leningrad, in the Baltic, when I visited it by ship, or Zanzibar, which is on the same longitude, and which I visited by Dhow from Mombasa, Kenya, to Visakhapatnam, Andhra Pradesh, on the east coast of India, on the Bay of Bengal. In other words the only major areas or continents I haven't traveled are the Indian Ocean, Antarctica, and Central Asia, though admittedly I could spend a lifetime in South America, the Middle, East, Asia...

Years later, as I embarked in my first post-divorce, long-term relationship, my long-term girlfriend told me that she was having trouble distinguishing the close-calls I'd had from one another. Since she is an advertising executive and I worked in downtown Manhattan at the time, I opted to portray the nearly 30 data sets in an Xcel spreadsheet that we could both easily quantify. Since she is a naturally protective mother who often found our different risk tolerances quite jarring, and since her motto is "avoid death," that was the title I chose for a list of activities which often seemed to depict seeking out and confronting death:

#	Eric's life-changing brushes with life-ending experiences			Updated 6 Dec., 2017
	Description (short)	*Location (abbrev.) Italics = boat name*	*Month / Year*	*Notes*
	MORTAL / HIGH			
1	Man-Over-Board 16 min.	100 miles southeast of Block Isl., *Windriven*	Oct-99	hypothermic
2	Black-tip shark attack fm. 40'	Rangiroa, Fr. Polynesia, *Stornoway*	Feb-94	it bit swim ladder off
3	slid down stream bed, nearly off 200' cliff	Moorea, opposite Tahiti, *Stornoway*	Mar-94	we heard water in time
4	gored/grazed by bull, under right ribcage	alone for weeks, Edeby farm, Sweden	Jul-87	grazed only, leapt away
5	stuck under submerged	spring torrents, canoeing	Jul-78	Dad saved me

	canoe, panicked, dark	family, W.Virginia		
6	hurricane winds 2+ weeks, transAt	Bermuda-Belgium, *Chebec*, 21 days	Jun-91	67 knot wind/broke gauge
7	attempt injection of AIDS-ridden needle/s	Malawi border guards sought bribes held me	Apr-92	Swedes missed me/ran back
8	2 knife-to-throat attacks, Alfred, trans-At, *Chebec*	crossing Atlantic Bermuda-Belgium	Jun-92	Paula said don't make mess
	SCARY / MEDIUM			
9	yacht caught fire, burned, sank	*Stiarnarna*, Chaguaramas, Trinidad	Jan-00	rescued by tug, Coast Guard
10	train John & I were on was hit by truck	Macedonia, Balkans	Aug-91	stuck aboard 1 day
11	double assault, attempted robbery	Dodoma, Tanzania bus plaza	Apr-92	fought off 2 guys

12	gas leak/yacht, stove nearly blew up, burned eyes/voice	*Mag. F.*, Charleston-Beaufort	May-03	hatches were open
13	lightning bursts surrounded yacht	*Anore*, Bermuda-Newport, intense	Jun-99	we fled, turbo
14	Tiger-shark attacked boat, I ran, lost balance	*Chebec* arriving Bermuda, hit 2 X	May-91	it hit front, back
15	botched plane landing, due buzzards on strip	Gallon Jug, Belize, tiny plane/strip	Nov-03	tilted wheels up to avoid
16	Queen's Birthday Storm, arrival Auckland, NZ	Tonga-NZ, 3 sank, 3 KIA, *Stornoway*	May-94	arrived start of storm

Fortunately, not all of these close calls resulted in scars, otherwise this would be more than a booklet.

The list continues:

	RISKY / LOW			
17	1st landfall of Hurricane Andrew, Harbour Isl., Bahamas	stuck in wood house shook like hell, debris	Aug-92	no serious injuries
18	car crash, bit of blood, ditch, Africa	Arusha, central Tanzania, East Africa	Apr-92	no serious injuries
19	concussion from schoolground fight	St. Andrew's School, Nassau c. age 12	Nov-82	scalp wound, blood
20	arrested, Panama, ghetto, early AM	brothel district, for our own safety	Dec-93	cops drove us *Stornoway*
21	assaulted, King's Cross, Sydney, OZ	I'd been chatting with abuser's girlfriend	Nov-94	wounded pride
22	facing down Road Trains, Outback	Cairns-Ayers Rk/Outback, 1 lane/huge truck	Jul-89	insane drops roadside
23	solo mountain drive, Mexico	Guadalajara-Puerto Vallarta	Feb-07	winding roads, v. fatigued

24	cut 6" prop line/pen knife at sea	off Cape Cod Canal week before wedding	Oct-03	hit by prop/shaft, head/face
25	yacht dragged ashore in storm	anchorage, Cuttyhunk MA, yacht *Babe*	Sep-00	tied off, govt buoy
26	hit large chimpanzee while driving	rented car Seletra-Johor, Malaysia	Apr-97	we saw it limping
27	landed on burning runway, Es Salvador	El Salvador airport tarmac grass afire	Nov-12	1st we diverted to Managua

Note: One of the scariest episodes was being hit by a Thai long boat some 17 years before this list was tabulated; yet it didn't even make it into this list... what else was left out?

This short book will be published on my fiftieth birthday. In preparation, my publishing colleagues and I tabulated and re-bound 8,000 photographs into seven volumes. Then a team of dozen typists in many time zones typed 53 diaries into a single, 733-page hard-cover bound book for my son and I. Then I started a memoir, optimistically entitled *First Fifty*.

This book is very personal. The content is very revealing. But I'm alright with that; I've been publishing autobiographical articles since my teens, and books since my 30's. Gradually, over 30 years, I've worked, often anonymously, as an advocate for victims of child sex abuse, and openly against predators and the phalanx of "reputable" persons and organizations who enable them.

Photographer Caitlin and I are hopeful that this book, small yet revelatory, will appeal to a fresh, new demographic, accustomed to body art, adornment, and celebrating one's body, its many flaws and all. After all, our imperfections tell stories: of joy, of anger, self-harm, and of a desire for a time, however painful, to be remembered; literally etched on our bodies.

On Monday the 14th of March, 1988, I was 17 years old and in boarding school outside Newport, Rhode Island. I had just returned from a choir tour of the UK, and was about – though I didn't realize it at the time – to join forces with a female student and oust the school choir master for touching her boyfriend (and me). I sat in my cell-like rectangle of a room with a three-inch-high bedframe on the floor and so many mice that I fed and named them, and penned the following outline for this book:

Basis for a Poem on Scars

> Scars – place on body, how gotten.
> Written romantically, poetically.

Tells of E.T.W.'s [my] body scars necessary.

Original concept, imaginative – has potential.

For example:

    Slash across right knee, left to right. Early-age baseball, sliding into the fence.
    The "Y"-shaped scar on the thumb on my right hand. An "eternal question," as asked by Julian Sands in Room With A View, with Denholm Elliott, by Merchant & Ivory. Weeding grass with a machete in the laundry area. Early shame, blood.
    A few weeks before, on Tuesday, 1 March, 1988, I had lain the groundwork for this collection by making the following *Scars Tally*: For the first half dozen or so scars I actually annotated symbols for what the scars looked like, as though they would somehow vanish before I wrote the book:

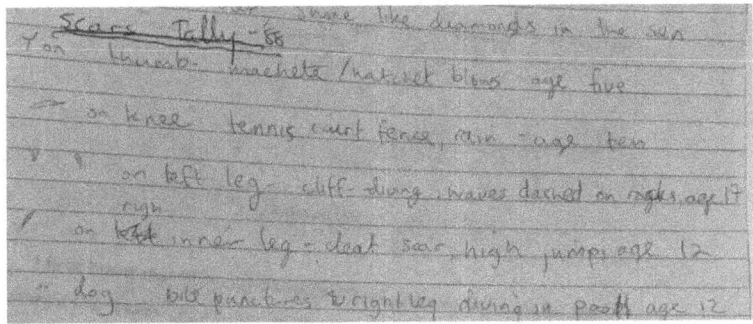

Scars Tally, Age 17:

"Y" on thumb – machete, hatchet blows, age 5
" ---- " on knee, tennis court fence, rain, age 10
" \\   // " on left leg, cliff-diving, waves dashed on rocks, age 17
"U" on right inner leg, cleat, from high jump, St. Andrew's School, Nassau, age 12

- " @ @ " dog bite punctures, right leg, diving in pool, age 12
- Pock-mark scars, cuts, left hand, football, as a lineman versus Rivers Academy, junior varsity, linebacker, age 17
- Knuckle scars, from punching walls and doors, school & home etc. ages 16-17
- Inner left arm – large infection scars, age c.10
- Chicken pox and impetigo scars (we got golf balls and turtles from ponds badly polluted by sewage and industrial laundry outflow from hotels near home)
- Left foot, sailing, early teens
- Stomach, right side, surfing on cracked board, age 17
- Left wrist – bathing, nude, swimming in icy water of the Arctic Circle, in a clear river, camping through Scandinavia with brother, 1987
- Left eyebrow, hammer blow when young, age 5
- Chin scars – Jr. Varsity football, St. George's & Eaglebrook (boarding) schools, 13-18

What does any of this tell us? That since my mid-teens I have been fascinated with the subject-matter, with what we each try to tell ourselves about our bodies, how we alter our bodies to effect the way people react to us (from hair, to weight, to overall appearance, including how victims of child sex abuse – or adult sexual assault – may try to de-beauty, or harm themselves to that perpetrators will not be attracted to them, or as a misguided form of self-punishment for their beauty having betrayed them.

Some of the material in this book may be troubling. But that is part of the raw charm, the *víscera* of this booklet, and the message it is trying to convey. It's alright to reveal a bit about our bodies, they are us, not a "part," of us. We should be proud of ourselves and what each of us has been through. And perhaps others might even find it of interest.

Prepare to be regaled about the time someone killed a needlefish with a flake of rust from a wrecked Japanese long-linger on a Tongan atoll, ...then uses the same fishes' needle to extract a toxic bit of rust from his knee, embedded from falling in the rush to catch the fish!

Above all, thank you for being willing to open the pages of a booklet with such a large, jarring word for a title. We hope that you will be pleased.

E. T. W.
East Boston, MA
August, 2020

Part I: Shame Scars

Short story:

I first burnt myself during boarding school, while having a smoke alone in a jungle-like thicket known to students as Vietnam. It would prove the first of several brandings. Like rings on a tree, I have imprinted these phantasms of pink tissue across my body, from ankle to eye. Sealed within each is a smoky, elusive feeling. An emotion encapsulated. A passion, and a shame, both pleasure and pain.

My first burn seemed out of place on an otherwise unblemished body. Really, I felt as out of place as a burn in a school which was meant to be like a family. I conspired the burn on a warm spring afternoon. The humid air clung to me like an accomplice. I was utterly and secretively alone. Everyone else was at sports practice; either girls' field hockey or boys' lacrosse. Their shouts drifted towards me across an old wooden racquetball court and through dense underbrush.

They didn't bother me. I'd gained exemption from sailing in order to write. The jungle felt private around me. I sat on my haunches in the depths of Vietnam; our own no-man's-land. The breeze wafting in from the New England coast was unusually warm. I hadn't long to wait before summer released me. It would be my fifth and final summer break from boarding school. Then, the autumn after next, I would no longer be welcomed back. I'd had these thoughts before.

Distractedly, I scanned my bare shoulders, noticing a little red pimple on the freckled side of my right arm. My eyes fell like the tongues of bells, examining my torso, a taught undulating navel, my crotch, protruding knees embossed in light hair, my worn shoes....

I looked over my shoulder, away from my smoke. Birds rustled from winter's lethargy. Worms writhed in a moist caviar of soil.

The pimple again. I could see it plainly, but couldn't feel it. It depressed me more than the empty bottles (which I hadn't helped to drink) that lay scattered around me in the rotting, throbbing silence.

My cigarette began to burn low.

I smoke with my left hand; it was all I could rub my right arm with. I scratched the welt. Nothing. I squeezed it. Nothing. Then I felt a sting of fire as my lit cigarette brushed against it. A tinge of pain rippled through me. I found it disturbing, yet vaguely pleasurable. The cigarette seemed like a numbing syringe; a cure.

Before crushing my spent cigarette in the butt-littered soil, I took a fresh, slender smoke out of its box and lit it with the old. Dabbing a fingertip in saliva, I slavered my warm spit around the pimple and blew on it gently. It tingled cool as it dried, leaving my skin caked in thin, bubbly ridges. Then it seemed to ripen, stretching outwards.

Deliberately and steadily, I pressed the cigarette against my flesh. At first, the heat itched in a teasing, insinuating way. Then it stung painfully. Then dully. I clenched my lower lip between my teeth. It curled the circle of skin into a thin, papery film. Pale and drained at first, it soon swelled up and away from the sinews beneath, like an airy blister.

I closed my eyes.

I hadn't expected to feel, as I clawed my way out of Vietnam towards the dormitories, a mild sense of elation. But I did. The raw burn clung uncomfortably to my T-shirt, but I thought of it as a wedding band; a pact with myself. It would scar. We were united till death. I crawled my way out of this proving-ground feeling much more together; much more me. I had my own little secret.

Though I determined to hide it from the old man in the dormitory, I also knew that I never could. Two nights later, with the light of the moon filtering through motionless curtains, his fingers ran across it and stopped.

He worried about it, this dorm-master of mine; wanted to report it. But smoking is illegal, and only a smoke could have caused that dusty-green, concentric blister. He couldn't declare it without indicting himself. The nurse might ask 'What was he doing brushing my bare arms?,' or 'Why was he letting me smoke?' Unlike my body, and my writings (which he would sift through while I was in class), it remained my own scar - not his.

Me and my filthy body. All the less reason for him to touch me.

When they finally booted my dorm-master a few weeks later, after they finally did ask 'What were you doing, holding boys in your rooms long after lights out?' and 'Where has so-and-so been all this time?' I felt liberated. Giddy with the thrill of release, cognizant that I had been living under a smothering of condoned lies for two years, I wanted more than anything to run away.

Gazing at it daily, I wanted to run away to sea. Our school overlooked the shore, proudly straddling a peninsula on the rugged New England coast. Though its chapel loomed defiantly, the grounds slid gently down a long hill towards a ream of stone cliffs, the gentle sand, and the North Atlantic... towards Africa.

At night, between study hall and lights out, I would walk along the hill, nestle against the wall, roll a cigarette for myself, and gaze longingly across the dark line of its surface. Dimly lit, boats would push outwards over the Continental Shelf and away.

The long, sultry afternoons alone made me feel that much dirtier. I would don a winter outfit and skateboard down the main avenue, through the stone gates, and behind the backyards of faculty homes to the scraggy coast. There, I would scrape off most layers of my clothing and sprawl out to read. Often, one of the girls' teams would come puffing past, recognize me,

and perhaps hail. Mostly they would look away, trying to conceal their
exhaustion, which is never easy when you're out of breath.

I tired of these routines before long, and with the spring rains began writing in earnest. Meanwhile, the ice had melted off the mooring lines of the sailboats in nearby Newport harbor. One by one, they cast off and set sail. I knew the crew and destinations of some of them, and even helped push off one of them for my ancestral Sweden. I longed to stow aboard, and strained my eyes for them many nights afterwards.

Then, inevitably, summer came again and, with it, vacation.

One of the first things I learned, while bussing tables in a restaurant overlooking the harbor that summer, is that the biennial Newport to Bermuda Race would begin on June 15. I will never forget that date. June 15. I etched it first in my mind. My body would come later. The first I heard of the race, heard of the demand for young, healthy, prep-school boys like myself, I began secretly to anticipate it.

I wanted a berth aboard one of more than a hundred yachts mustering for the occasion. Neither wages nor victory inspired me. It was the thought of finally, really, escaping; across the Gulf Stream to Bermuda. I hit the docks advertising myself at every opportunity for weeks. I wrote my own flyers and 'business cards' with a black felt marker, reading "eager student, healthy, 17 years, hoping to crew in

Bermuda Race - have sailed offshore before, can clean, cook..." I photocopied, posted, and handed out dozens of them.

I got to know a range of skippers and crew, boat-bums and yachties. Some treated me warmly to an anecdote and maybe a beer, others to disdain and evasive lies. Most listened patiently to sumNancys of my sailing in the Baltic and Caribbean. None of them gave me a berth.

Around me, other prep-school kids; kids with parents who summered on Long Island Sound, kids who'd been raised with a tiller in their palm and a pennant above their heads, were offered berths. They were friends of friends of skippers or crew. Everyone else seemed to be, or become, on the 'inside'.

"Looking for a cook on Bermuda race", a posting would say. What they didn't say is that they were looking for a woman cook. Or better, a girl. I winced.

On the morning of the race I woke slowly from a tired, sad sleep. There was an anvil pressing against my heart. In over three weeks of trying, I hadn't found a boat. The first gun would send boats hurtling southward at noon. It was foggy and gently chilly. I wanted to spend the day enshrouded in such a fog.

I figured I would be safely insulated from the race in the garden shed of a bed-and-breakfast several avenues up from the harbor. I'd accepted a long-standing invite from a schoolmate named Roger to return with him to the shed in which he lived and get high. Roger, known as Rod, had been brought to school from Pittsburgh on a hockey scholarship. He never had, and never would, fit in there. The worst part was that he believed he could. Rod had changed. The school hadn't. And it wouldn't. We were both working on recovering from school, each in our own, quiet way.

Rod woke me at around mid-morning. For a while I lay in a cot set against the corrugated siding and watched him fawning over his plants. He sat on the edge of the bed adjusting a plastic pot of Geraniums. He gave each of his flowers names, and would talk to them softly. They were his only companions. He had given me a pot which I named George the Geranium. I had cared for George dutifully, thinking of Rod when I watered it, as he probably hoped I would. He was talking to a light-green pot of flowers which he called Samantha.

Putting Samantha down, Rod jostled my feet, calling me to join him for the left-overs of the guests' breakfast. From where we ate quietly in the kitchen, I could see and overhear one of the guests. There, in the coffee room, resting after breakfast, was the kind of woman who I could only envision being the parent of a prep-school kid. She was sipping her tea with a companion hidden from my view. They were talking about their husbands. Soon, the woman's companion began urging her, saying how they really ought to go down to the harbor. Their husbands would be pushing off for Bermuda before noon, and they really ought to be getting along to see them off. Did they have enough film?

After they had set off, Rod and I plodded warily towards Newport Harbor. Though we dragged our heels, we soon found ourselves swept up in pre-race fervor. There would be staggered starts throughout the afternoon. The first start gun was a mere hour away when we made the docks, that apron between land and sea where no one was purely spectator. There are last-minute provisions to be shuttled aboard, racing forms to be signed and submitted, farewells to be said, and boats to be cast off from the dock. Cast off by standby's like me and Rod; by supposed landlubbers.

Rod, the gardener, quickly tired of the intensity, the orders being yelled and obeyed. I couldn't draw myself away. Nor could I resist, while casting a boat off or helping the skipper aboard, asking quietly if they needed an extra crew. The responses were either laughter or surprise. Everyone really seemed to have their shit together. This was big-time racing, I was told. Still, I'd been carrying my passport and some cash with me for days - just in case.

By twenty minutes before noon, docks previously overloaded were suddenly vacant. All the sailboats had pushed off. All but one. What happened during the next quarter hour went by so quickly that the final gasp of time and the night following it are difficult for me to recall. All I know is that sometime late the following morning I woke with the anvil still on my heart and a hand that I hardly recognized as my own, it was burned so badly.

Twenty minutes to noon found me lounging on the dock with some other left behinds preparing to own up to my failure. I was pretending to scoff nonchalantly at the crew of the only remaining boat, who were dashing about and calling frantically. In truth, I was watching them closely.

The skipper stood on the dock before me, rasping demands at a stocky, quiet fellow who looked like a winch-grinder . The skipper dashed past me to the phone. He punched a number. He asked a question. He hung up and prepared to stomp past me again. I asked him if I could help. Bulb-headed, brow-knit and intense, he looked at me irritably, took two steps, stopped, and flung his face in mine.

"You sail?"

"Why, y-y-yes," I stammered.

"Talk to him," he said, pointing at the big, mild-mannered guy, "That's Jim. He's the mate."

Confused, even nervous, I stumbled towards Jim. Suddenly interested, he strode towards me.

"You sail?" he asked critically.

Again, "Yes". My ego began to kick in.

"Yes I sail. You've probably read about me. Those are my flyers," I said, pointing at the board above the telephones. I warmed to my theme. "I've sailed before. Never been seasick. I've been trying to get aboard all month. I really want to go. I love to sail. I've cleaned plenty of boats.... I cook..."

"You cook?"

"Sure - Swedish pancakes for breakfast, rice at night...."

"Captain Phillips - I think we've got one!," he called out. He scampered back to his skipper, who was rasping at his wife. They talked. The mate called out "Got your passport?" liked my reply, and asked me for it. I rarely give my passport to anyone, but I did. While they regrouped and scratched out all kinds of forms - waiver forms for a crew member who never showed up - I rushed to settle my own accounts. By then it was about ten minutes to twelve. They weren't due to start till one, but all boats had to submit forms and push off by noon.

My hands literally shaking at the turn of events, at the prospect of signing aboard and pushing off for Bermuda momentarily, I struggled out a few sentences to those remaining. One of them could borrow my bike if he took my key and left it at my apartment, telling my room-mates where I'd gone. An acquaintance who was eager for work could have my job as bus-boy. My next shift began at four. I scribbled a note to my boss explaining my departure. Two minutes to twelve.

"Kid, we're off!" It was the skipper. "Bye Hon' - get these forms in," he was telling his wife and leaning towards her as I prepared to scramble aboard.

Then there was a commotion behind me. A noisy hammering of a truck horn. The rolling of gates along unoiled tracks. The screeching of tires. The yelling of someone's name, both from the deck of the boat and from behind me, where the compound was erupting in cheering. One foot on the boat, the other on the dock, I turned around.

A thin man in his early thirties, with a mop of dirty blond hair, was literally hurtling over sailing dinghies and abandoned gear towards us. He was carrying a week's supplies of sailing gear, boots in one hand, a canvas bag in another. A sailor. He leapt onto the floating dock, threw the mate his gear, and slid beneath the lines and onto the deck.

Then he just lay there, panting.

The skipper looked up as he leaned over the railing. His unaccountable crew; the sailor he had contracted to win the race, was suddenly accountable. The time was noon. He looked at me. I still didn't get it. He shook his head with a genuine sadness, took back the forms from his wife and nodded her towards me with a meaningful look. I started to get it. A plunger was swelling in my throat. The skipper pulled his weight backwards, away from me.

"I'm sorry," he whispered. His wife handed me back my passport.

"Cast off!" They did. I almost fell into the harbor as they yanked away. I wish I had. The last thing I saw as they hoisted sail were scraps of paper; a waiver form with my name on it torn to shreds, floating silently in their wake. The heavier ones had already begun to sink when I turned my back.

The burning in my throat wouldn't melt the lump that has just swelled there. I figured Black Seal Bermudian rum might do better. I had three of them straight in the nearest bar before I even began to realize what had just happened. A succession of drinks and cigarettes later, and I had spent most of my cash intended for the bars of Bermuda.

When I sensed my shift at the restaurant looming, I looked at myself in the mirror across the bar, crumpled my notice of quitting, tossed it into the ashtray, drained my final glass, assembled my gear, and lay my right hand, palm-down upon the bar. What was left of my Marlboro cigarette, I punched downward on the back of my palm, causing the veins there to strain outward, and bringing an involuntary moisture to my eyes. Smearing the butt forcibly, I watched its last sparks wither and choke against my sweet flesh.

The smoke cleared. It was out.

The bartender tried damn hard to seem as though he wasn't looking at me. He wasn't looking at me anyway. He was looking at my hand. I put the cigarette butt in the ashtray on top of my note and walked out.

Between the bar and work I managed a shave, cutting myself more times than I care to remember. The worst cut was at the fleshy base of my nose. During my shift, I served my clients with the burn on my hand swollen grotesquely and blood caked under my nose. At that rate, I wouldn't need notice of quitting in order to lose my job.

When I knocked off after the dinner shift, there was only a dull throb left of me. I staggered back to the same stool in the same bar that I had first gone to that afternoon, picking up a pack of non-filter Chesterfield cigarettes along the way. Before the late-night crowd had arrived, I had downed another pair of straight rums. Before I'd finished my third one, I again lay down my right hand, palm down on the bar.

The barman looked away.

This time there would be no punching. This time I let my Chesterfields, the classic smoke, do the work for me. It burned slowly; fresh hair first, leaving wisps of fragrant smoke. This time I actually enjoyed watching the welt form beneath the ashen remnants. At the very least, I felt no pain.

Then I went on smoking the same cigarette.

I didn't have a friend in the bar, and was starting to wonder how much longer I could last when a young woman claimed the cramped stool beside mine. She was visiting from Boston, she told me, reminding me that it was a weekend. Though I can't remember her name, she reminded me a lot of my older sister, and so II think of her as being named Beth.

While I was lighting a cigarette for her , Beth found the glowing welts, which I had been hiding under my left palm. In slow, but deliberate clumps of words, I tried to explain, to justify my state of mind; my state of body. She listened, rapt.

I remember that Beth hadn't finished her first drink before rubbing the welts with ice, in the same way that tears were rubbing my eyes with salt. It would take more than ice to soothe a deep, burning pain, but every bit of soothing helped.

While Beth made her way out of the bar, a fleet of sailboats were making their way towards the Gulf Stream, and a fleet of sordid aspirations were beginning to forge themselves into burnings which would riddle my body during the years to come, from ankle to eye.

Photo: Despite having been kicked off it at the start of the race from Newport to Bermuda, I was able to find a berth on a boat from Bermuda back to Newport, so when *Flyway* finished their race, to their surprise there was the kid they threw out with the trash, camera and writing quill in hand!

Part II: Head

Horse:

Scar on scalp, left side above ear, from being thrown from horse at Camperdown Riding Stable in Nassau, Bahamas, head hit barrel, 1987, age 7. This riding school is on Wild Tamarind Drive off Eastern Road, New Providence, and, as older sisters are wont to be, my sister was (and is) into horses and horse riding. My parents obliged the three boys as well with riding lessons (they are cool that way, offering break dancing lessons later). So uncertain was I in a saddle that as we approached a barrel around which I was meant to steer the horse (or pony), it balked, slammed on its brakes (or hooves), and I kept going, over its mane and against the edge of the barrel.

I received a cut which bled slightly, and I think some disinfectant and ice; not stitched. It gradually healed, invisible due to my hair, only reminding me of it during periodic skin cancer checkups, or the few times I've shaved bits of my head, mostly for swimming championships, or rebellion. Since it was one of my first scars, I remember it.

It turns out that this fall from a horse was prescient. In fact, I am such a poor horseman that I have been literally been awarded 'dusty belly' awards more than once; at Camp Rockmont in the Black Mountains of the Carolinas, they give boys who fall off horses those cheap feather dusters that French maids in the *Playboy* cartoons use to sweep the tops of picture frames. In all my limited horse riding experience; in Wyoming, Montana, California, Texas, North Carolina, Coral Harbor Bahamas, Belize, Canada, on farm horses in Sweden, even on camels in Australia (if that counts; there were Dromedary, outside Alice Springs), I have only proved any equestrian utility once: in Montana.

On the first day of a week in a decidedly low-key, informal, family ranch, my hosts were eagerly catching up with the wizened guide and ranch owner. On about the second hour of a 3-4 hour ride, the conversation amongst the four other adults was still intense (they had decades and generations and years apart to catch up on). For whatever reason, as we left the woods and were walking (the slowest speed for riding) along the long ridge of a gently sloping, whale-back-shaped hill. Ahead of us, for many miles, was a valley with mountains in the far distance. It was partly cloudy and still where we were, but about a mile away I watched as dense grey clouds spilled over the ridges of the mountains, and rapidly filled the valleys below. Something was afoot.

Then I noticed that ahead of the quick-moving clouds and mist was thick bands of rain, and in the July heat the friction created intense lightning activity ahead of it. I openly admit that I know very little about the great outdoors, about mountains and their weather systems, and even less about Montana, horses, or how to ride them. But as a sailor with tens of thousands of miles spent on tropical seas on small boats, I felt that I understood lightning, squalls, rainstorms, and microbursts to react; as one must react on a sailboat and go from lackadaisical to urgent in seconds.

"Sir," I called out to the lead cowboy, who I had only met that day; "I don't know much, but in my opinion, that in front of us is some serious lightning, and I'm not sure we want to be on a ridge when it hits."

"Holy shit!" he muttered when he recognized our predicament, "Everyone off the ridge – to the treeline down there, NOW!" he yelled, calmly but firmly as they say.

Well, there are several steps one should take to go from lackadaisical to urgent on a horse, or so I had been told: using stirrups or spurs and reins and voice and maybe even a crop, one is supposed to develop acceleration in this manner: from a walk to a trot, then to a canter, and finally a gallop. Of course, we all just went straight into a gallop! Remember, I'm no horseman, and there were innumerable prairie dog holes littering the landscape, but somehow I managed to keep up with the group without being thrown, catching a hoof in a hole or experiencing some other calamity. We hitched the horses to tree branches and huddled under a tree together as the heavy rain and lightning struck us moments later.

I like to think I redeemed my dusty feather awards, being barrel-tossed, and the butt of equine humor. Just that once. I've since hung up my spurs.

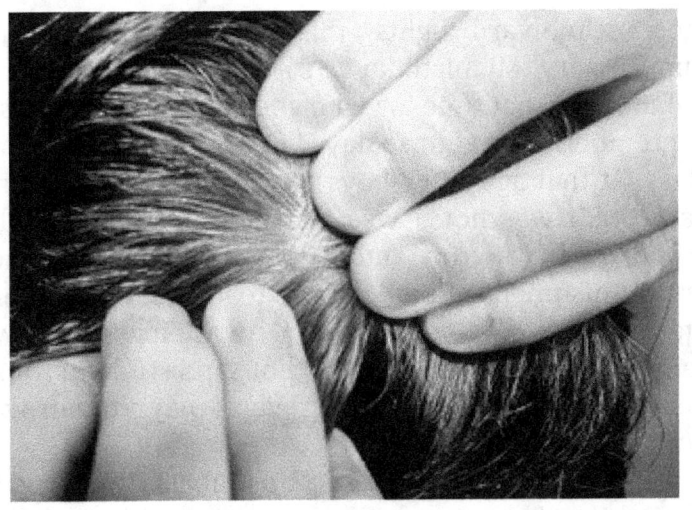

Photo: Scalp, showing results of yet another failed equine mis-adventure.... Some of us never learn.

Diary entry seven years later; August 10, 1987:

"I am on a train from Stockholm to Göteborg. I was, however very apt at being social and friendly, and also won all but one of many fights, yet not the one where I attacked Roger from behind. He is tall and skinny and fell backwards, giving me a bloody concussion at St. Andrew's."

Fight:

Photo of scar from schoolyard fight with Roger at St. Andrew's School in 1981, age 11; concussed. Like most schoolyard fights, this one was stupid and unnecessary. My birthday is 27 August. The cut off in Bahamas at that time for who goes in what class was 1 September. So by 3 or so days I was the youngest in my class. At that age some boys were hitting puberty and very big. I was not; I was considerably smaller. The school I left was tiny and intimate; the only violence was punishment of students by teachers, not student on student. The new school was massive: two campuses, from K to 12, like a thousand students, or so it seems. Bad behavior in the several playgrounds was not uncommon.

    I guess the school was "US Embassy-approved," something businesses from apartment renters to others strive to obtain. There were dozens of students who were the children of US Embassy staff, with all kinds of colorful backgrounds and countries they had lived in. Several lived near the "Marine House" which was close to our house, and I befriended one of the boys, named Paul, from Michigan. Paul became a football lineman, affable, rotund, with large glasses, we got along well. Later, a tall skinny Embassy son enrolled at the school, and moved next to Paul, so naturally they also became friendly. I recall sneaking out of the house to go to the casino during overnights, and exploring the neighborhood, though Paul was not as woodsy as we were. We thoroughly searched a home which had burned and made a very upsetting discovery – a baby human's skull in a bag in what had been the attic.

Anyway, it was not uncommon for Paul to provoke me into antagonizing other kids by feeding me basically false information; one poor boy this involved whether he was circumcised or not. Because I was younger and smaller I was susceptible to such manipulation. To up the tension, Paul campaigned for me to pick a fight with Roger. I still don't know why. I am sure Roger was not in on it. But sure enough Paul worked me into such a state that with about 5 minutes before the end of mid-day break, I confronted Roger over some perceived slight and challenged him to a fight. I barely came up to his elbows – I would say he was about 6' and I was about 4'. But I persisted and got in his grill, with Paul behind me, and ultimately insulted and baited him so much in front of other people that he had no choice really than to walk into a "bowl" created by delivery bays, that created a small amphitheater of sorts.

You know what happened next; the chant of "fight, fight, fight" broke out and with no faculty around to do anything about it the "stadium" filled with over 100 or so spectators and Roger and I circled each other. All he had to do was hold his arm out and I could not get near him. He kept saying

"Don't do this, Eric, we don't have to do this."

Well, I persisted, and though I don't think I connected any kind of harmful punch on Roger, ultimately he was forced (and I honestly never could blame him), to hit me. Well, I was thrown to the ground by the hit, and kind of dazed. I recall many loud cheers for Roger, jeers and general commotion (I don't think I was very popular at the school). Then Roger did something that he didn't realize I could see; he turned his back from me and raised his arms in triumph. This did two things; it humiliated and angered me, and it also gave me a clean shot at him for the first time in the fight; his entire back was exposed to me, with no fists to beat me away.

    I got up, ran a couple steps towards him and then jumped onto Roger's back, grabbing his neck with both my arms. I was 11 or 12 and only about 100 pounds but Roger was very tall and skinny, and completely taken by surprise by this assault. Understandably off balance, and by the laws of physics top-heavy, we both fell to the ground. You can imagine which way we fell, right? Backwards!

    I hit my head in the pavement at a pretty high rate of speed, and with the combined weight of Roger and me – probably over 250 pounds – falling from 6 feet up, I understandably received a cut to the back of my head. I was light blonde at the time, and our uniforms were white short-sleeved Oxford shirts. I bled like a stuck pig, and it was quite a sight. The bell rang to end recess, still not a single adult in sight – we never did see one – and so some classmates, including Roger, picked me up and ran me about a quarter mile around the large gym, under the overpass, past the middle school classrooms which were all open to the outside with faded brown wooden slats for windows, so that my younger brother James could see me being carried limp, on my back, by four other boys, my head hanging backwards, blood all over, me passed out.

We told the nurse I'd fallen down the stairs. Roger never got in trouble that way, nor did I. The teachers remained (until today) ignorant.

I was diagnosed with a concussion and sent home to recover for a few days. On Friday or Saturday our friend Heather hosted a nice garden get-together for friends (I recall Andrew, Tim, Frank, Remo, Paul, Shana, Leslie, Melanie, Tiffany, and others). I showed up feeling sheepish, and folks were solicitous of my health and the guys of course wanted to see the stitches and learn about concussions and scars and bleeding and things.

I think the one most traumatized was my younger brother; there were many ways to get to the nurse's office, and I wish they hadn't carried me past his classroom - he was about age nine at the time. Even though he saw me looking half-dead, head lolling round, it my hair and shirt covered in blood, he wasn't allowed to get up and help or find out what happened to his older brother.

At Heather's party there was an awkward moment when Roger arrived, and the small group of children let out an audible little gasp. But I was relieved to make peace with him, as he was with me; we shook hands and did one of those awkward chest bumps, and I told him it wasn't his fault, I wasn't upset.

From that point I believe both Roger and I realized that Paul wasn't such a great friend to either of us.

Pop-Up:

On my first day of boarding school in Western Massachusetts, classmate Tony pushed me into Tom's head during a game of pop-up, in which Mr. Janes a US Navy veteran of Vietnam, rumored to have also been in intelligence, hit a red ball high in the air with a bat and a dozen or so boys scrambled to be the one who caught it.

Because it was a violent shove (I still don't know if Tony caught the ball), my front top teeth embedded in the back scalp belonging to Tom. Since this both caused him pain and drew blood, it also drew all the attention to him, and made me look like the bad guy who caused it – of course I could not see who pushed me. The impact killed my right front tooth, meaning all the nerves were severed and it became "dead." Ironically, since the nerve died, the experience was quite painful.

I took my first trip to Greenfield where a dentist tested it with electricity – also painful – and confirmed it was over. He later carved out the back of the tooth, took out anything that might infect, put in a metal rod and sealed it up. Aside from minor discoloration, this worked wonderfully for about 30 years, when a dentist in Greenwich Connecticut re-sealed it. For our wedding photos I was told to have it bleached, so I did, though it later got darker again.

Interestingly, Tom's mother represented PeeWee Herman, his cousin was my boss at a Newport restaurant and later a realtor, and another cousin became a good friend. The family are well known, with several popular documentaries made about them. Tony went on to become first my roommate and then on the losing side of what is considered the worst beat-down in mixed-martial arts in the US.

Thai long boat:

Photo: I took this of a Thai speedboat known as a long boat, with gasoline-powered truck engines strung on long poles to a propeller in a wire mesh cage. It is off Rai Lay Bay near Ao Nang, Krabi Province, and the fellow in the front left of the boat is Thomas A., a Norwegian friend from Singapore years.

Photo: A long boat making a rapid approach from between several islands. Because the shafts do not go deeply into the water, they are harder to hear underwater than most drive-unit outboard motors in the "west."

From a log of my trip: Diary; Mid-February, 2001:

"The biggest scare of the Thailand trip was when I was literally run over by a 30-foot, 20-knot 'long boat' off Po Dan Island. I'd been submerged, snorkeling, for about 40 seconds, roughly 100 meters (300 feet) from the beach. When I surfaced I was stunned to see, with no audio or visual warning, the bow of this boat, with a 'bone in its teeth' (frothy waves) literally less than a meter from me and moving at least a meter a second. Fortunately, I managed to fend the bow off from my head (with my right forearm against its starboard bow), and dive.

Then I lay prone, four feet underwater, and waited for the props to chop over my legs. When that didn't happen, and after ten seconds or so of waiting, I surfaced in time to see the bastard driver sitting in the BOTTOM of his boat, not looking up, his view blocked by a dozen passengers. Angry and scared, I yelled sharply. No response. I yelled again. He was speeding away. But any friends on shore picked up on my alarm and began to swim out to help me. I was really shocked I traced the same boat returning from Chicken Island, got his details, and later that day was able to confront the captain with a Thai interpreter (another skipper), once back at Rai Lay Beach Bungalows.

My travel mates thought it was useless to do so, but I learned in shipping that 'silence is deadly', and that even near misses or 'incidents' (as opposed to accidents) should be discussed and circulated. Perhaps for a few weeks the skippers will be extra vigilant of swimmer; before relapsing to their lackadaisical ways... One hopes... I am quite sure that

1) he came very close to killing me (the bow would easily have stove in, or crushed, a person's head on impact), and that

2) had I not been raised around boats in Bahamas and worked on them for a living, I might not have (read: an average person might not have) been able to react as quickly and calmly as I did.

It was, after all, a classic 'deer in the headlights' scenario."

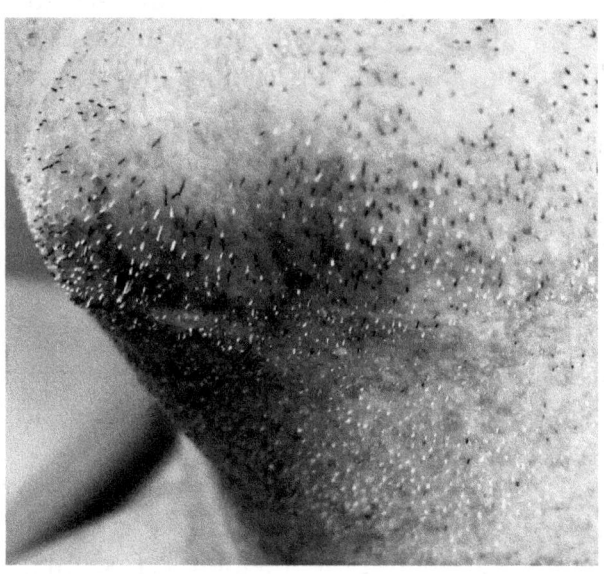

Photo: Unusual angle of rarely-seen scars on chin from American football and rugby.

Chin:

I have two scars under my chin from contact in football games. I played four years of American football; yes, unlike Rugby, which I also played in Boston, Singapore and Connecticut, it is the sport played with all the padding! At Eaglebrook I was a running back and linebacker, but at St. George's they needed fellows who weren't even that beefy on the line. So I was both linebacker and offensive lineman, played on all special teams and offence and defense, and called the plays for defense, so I basically played continuously – yet only managed to score three points during my entire career!

With that much contact, and since the chin-strap was not padded, hitting my chin on helmets and other hard items was inevitable, and once I cut a wound and it bled, it remained vulnerable the rest of the season. That's how I have two scars on my chin; through organized violence, but not much of a bother and they rarely open up while shaving.

Recollection: Diary, October 15, 1988:

"I have a scar under my chin from being hit by a helmet under my chin strap in football. ...Enough for one night. Soon St. George's shall re-request my presence there. Share. Otherwise I am troubled by the school law, or am I wrong? Do I actually have until midnight? Enough, away!"

Surgeries above neck, from diaries:

- September 5, 2006: 9:15 am, Westport, Connecticut. Mohs surgery.
- September 7, 2006: Norwalk Connecticut, Dr. Bender (dermatologist, partner of Dr. Kolenick). Others okay. Skin based cell. Dr. Mohs surgery goes around cleans it out lowest

incidence of re-occurrence (best cosmetic result). Date of my first Mohs surgery of three to lower lip. Sit for an hour. Westport.
- September 12, 2006: 2 pm, skin surgery appointment, in Westport in two hours.

Part III: Hands & forearms

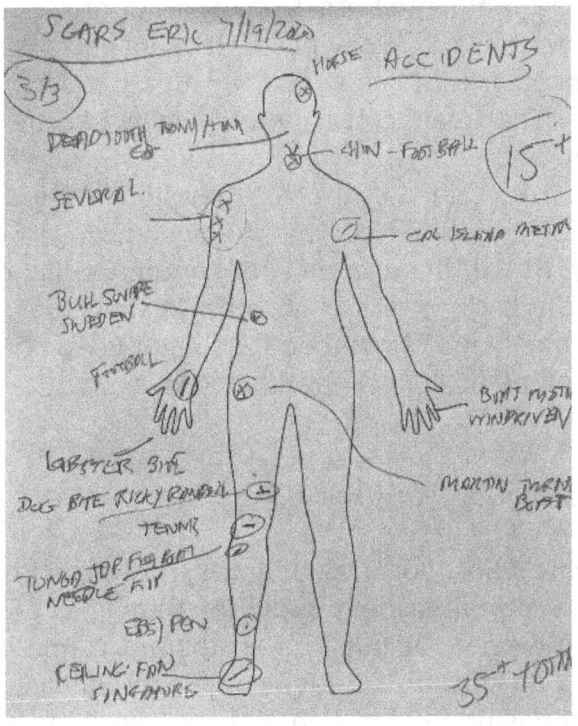

Photo: Sketch-chart of non-surgical, non-self-inflicted scars, 2020

Glass art, age 4: Diary; August 10, 1987:

"Reminiscing to earliest scars: "When I was very small my two brothers, my sister and I all went running into the bush. We were very young (about four years) and we broke bottles for the first time. We would pick up the pieces and play with them. We had never seen blood before. One of us cut ourselves and when we saw red, we wiped it. It came back. We were fascinated. It was a new trick, we didn't know pain.

We began cutting ourselves with the many broken bottles so that there was lots of red. We tried very hard to bleed as much as possible. After a while our laughs became curious whines and our German nanny, Nurse Ulla was shocked to find us. She rushed us to the bath, with lots of Dettol disinfectant, which stung like hell. I remember she taught us to cry at the sight of blood, which became our general reaction since."

Biking, age 14: Diary; April 20, 1985:

"In Eagle's Nest dorm, Eaglebrook, upstairs. I know I'll die in war. I think about girls a lot. Damn, I'm too shy, I haven't even made out. I swear too much, and I'm too lazy to do pushups. I have to get my hair cut soon. Sometimes I think I'm a spoilt brat. I wish my parents could see me play some of my sports. I hope I don't get slaughtered next year in *phubo* (football) I cut up my arm biking last Friday, before the dance."

Norwegian river, wrists, age 17:

Photo: The river near *Flåmsdalen* valley, Norway, where at age 17 brother John and I swam. Even in August there was still snow on the mountains and the rivers were, as you see, in high flow.

Diary; August 22, 1987:

"Joensuu, central, eastern Finland. My only injury this trip was of frightfully fatal potential. While jumping ass-first into the ice waters of the Flåm town's river on a Norwegian fjord (Bergen-Oslo) I ran my wrist across the jogged edge of a river rock. It drew a watery trickle of blood which was really of no worry, but the potential had definitely been there. During Thanksgiving break in my early teens we saw an acquaintance cut both of her wrists; she was drunk and she was extremely upset at her parents' divorce. So, only a year or so later, to see my own left wrist bleeding was a scare."

Photo: Older brother John cliff-diving into a fjord during our two-week backpacking and hitchhiking trip through Scandinavia in 1987. You can tell from the dry shorts and hair that this is his first dive – the navigational marker across the fjord suggests a high cliff dive.... I understand why our mother dislikes seeing images of our cliff and bungy-jumping!

Football, age 17: Diary; October 15, 1988:

"The Ark restaurant, on the corner of Memorial Boulevard and Thames Street, Newport [later the Red Parrot] …..My head throbs from being very warm, and my injured hand is bleeding again (I got a shallow strip of skin on my right thumb snacked on an opponent's football helmet or similar and it was stripped off about half a pencil-length but was slow to heal.) It was an almost-win game. I'm very bitter. We returned via bus by 6.30 pm this evening, I got a steak at school, and Mr. Tim Richards (my dorm master, young, informal, nice) drove me into town. Later: "My right hand's injury from the game versus Groton was reopened today; it, too, is ugly."

Forest behind home, Nassau, childhood, on arm: Diary; February 10, 1989:

"It snowed a few inches. I went to senior frostbite; a winter tradition. At night, I was reminded by a scar on my arm of childhood in a natural warm secure environment, of romping with my two brothers, while my sister did, well, we didn't know what our sister did. I would run around the Casuarina [whispering Australian pines] trees, naked and yelling, cooking, burning, stealing, finding, swimming: and in its own strange way, I have had to face that that is over. Jungle birds and shotgun pellet paths leading away rule my existence, coming together sometimes as I do now innocently. *Life is beauty; beauty is life. Art is beauty, beauty is art."*

Machete cut in shape of Why, *age 8: Diary; November 1, 1987:*

"St. George's; Two Why's: The *why* scar on my thumb and *why*? The eternal question. Accompanied by this drawing:"

Photo: Actual diary entry for November 1, 1987. It's like I have two right thumbs!

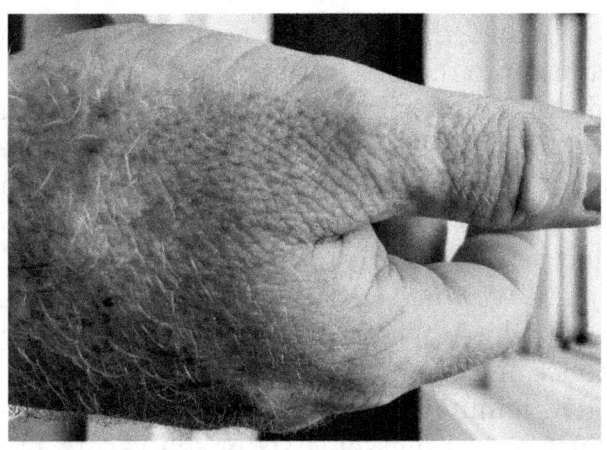

Photo: Y-shaped scar from childhood on right thumb, football scar on seam between smooth skin and pocked, and cigarette burn visible in inter as a lighter-colored circle.

Recalling the right-hand burning of Newport in 1990: Diary; June 19, 1990:

"I am in JFK International Airport, New York. For fifteen agonizing, tantalizing, nearly life-changing minutes, from 11:45 to 12 pm on *Flyway* (owned by O. P.), I was signed aboard for the race itself – ready to sail for Bermuda with passport and all, until the guy I was replacing showed up clumsily hungover flailing and yelling his way across the dock. My papers were torn up and tossed into the harbor, my dream of setting for Bermuda in moments dashed.

I untied the boat with a massive lump in my throat, went to the Ark bar, burned a large hole in the outside top of my right hand with a cigarette over shots of Bermudian Black Seal Rum by Gosling's, and went to work that night as a busboy at the Clarke Cooke House before I summarily quit the following day to join *Rising Star* and gave my bowtie to Tom P., my 92 Spring Street roommate who had worked there before. I may be staying on the beach perhaps tonight, though security and police on Bermuda are tough as hell! At 2.40 pm; I have five minutes before our descent to Bermuda. I have just picked out some six or ten yachts, out of a fleet of 137 contestants in the biennial Newport to Bermuda Race."

Diary; April 19, 1992:

"Room 20, Tusheries Lodge Guest House, Kilifi Harbor Village, north coast, Kenya. I depart for Dodoma in circa 1.5 hours, arriving 5 am, hopefully in time to connect with the 6 am bus to Arusha, where I plan to rest for one night before completing my full-fledged retreat from the grasp of the triumvirate frontiers of Zambia, Malawi, and Tanzania, with my tail between my legs.

My house of cards has collapsed by missing the boat, so my creed since June 17, 1990, after being ejected from the crew of the yacht *Flyway* racing from Newport to Bermuda by Mr. P., has been *never miss the boat*. He took my passport, signed me on board but threw the application in the water when a drunk crew ran to the boat late. I'd just been jettisoned from *Flyway* yacht and the Newport-to-Bermuda Race, my dreams spiked then crushed then tossed in the water. To enforce the memory, I slowly extinguished a cigarette on the top of my right hand at the Ark restaurant and bar that afternoon before a drunken last shift as bus-boy at the Clark Cooke House."

Photo: Taken by Captain Mike of me aboard the large racing yacht *Rising Star* looking at the burn to the outside of my right hand, about a week after the burn. We are sailing north from Bermuda, about to enter the Gulf Stream (note the onset of the mullet hair style!).

Failed trans-Atlantic voyage, cut hand on sail line, age 19: Diary; July 11, 1990:

"On voyage Bermuda to Lisbon, Portugal. The captain is to wake up R., which is lame. Now we got him up by yelling. Winds up. Helmed today. Then told me to do 'em tonight, *grrr*. Excuse the blood on opposite page, but I cut my hand while releasing the preventer on the jib sail (while jibing)."

Finger in engine, voyage to Carolinas, age, 28: Diary; October 18, 1999:

"Stripped tip of my left index finger nearly to the bone while (foolishly) testing an alternator fan belt on an offshore passage. We were approaching Cape Hatteras after several days of stormy weather in which I had been knocked overboard and morale and self-confidence was low. The injury happened when we lost all power except propulsion and basically headed to the nearest port in a barely subdued panic.

I was such a rookie at command in harsh weather with these complex boats that I mis-judged from over-filling the oil to thinking I would leverage fan belts off with wrenches. So when an alternator bolt was loose, potentially the reason we lost power, I tried to tighten it with my finger, which was quickly deeply stripped of its tip. Later in Charleston it was still bleeding so much that Gillian at City Marina had a van take me to the hospital to have it treated; the other captain in the van was dying to see the wound, so was the cab driver!

The voyage, with me as captain, Ajax as mate and a kids sailing coach named Daedalus, a young student from University of Rhode Island as crew. We left Newport bound for the Fort Lauderdale Boat Show via Morehead City, North Carolina, and Charleston aboard a 54-foot Little Harbor (aka Little Horror, per the graffiti in the stalls of the men who made them), named Windriven, formerly one of the Robins. The boats are perfect for what they are designed for the saying goes: "to get their owners into the fanciest yacht clubs."

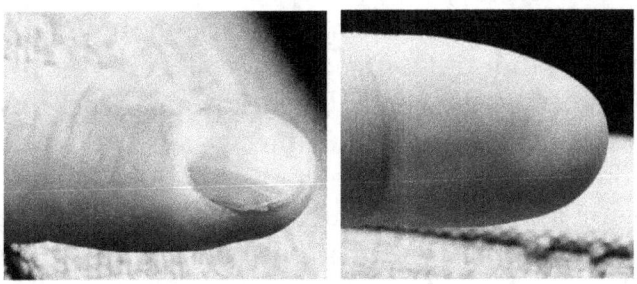

Photo: Left forefinger tip, stripped in the fan belt of the sailing yacht Windriven underway off the Carolinas in the fall of 1999 after the crew already went through a Man-Overboard incident. Out over nearly 150 offshore voyages, this counts as my worst. Subdued terror most of the time, wondering what part of boat, crew, or command (me) was going to break next.

Epilogue:

There is a very strange ending to this story; the voyage was supposed to take two weeks, but I was a relative rookie and it took over three, due to storms, breakages, delays, laying over in Morehead City and Charleston. Poor Daedalus; the penalties he was getting from parking tickets were almost as much as his wages and he was having a terrible time watching met and the boat getting beat up from mishaps, falling over, and having to hear the brokers yelling at me to get going. At the Blind Tiger bar in Charleston he was so drunk his head would lie on the bar and he would just mumble, only very rarely raising it to look up.

Meanwhile, back in Rhode Island, and unknown to us at the time, Daedalus' college ex-girlfriend registered that he would be back from a work voyage in two weeks, so sometime during the third week she put out a rumor that Dave had sexually assaulted her .As soon as Daedalus, about age 20, went to his friends place near Kingston for a beer on returning over a week later, several young men, including the nephew of a very close friend of mine, took him aside. They were beginning to administer a memorable lesson for having sexually assaulted their friend. Very soon thereafter my cell phone rang. It was my friend's nephew, who I will call ZZ:

"Hi, Eric, (heavy breathing and background noise: "Do you know a guy named Daedalus at URI?"

"Yes, I do, why?" I'd just paid him out and was enjoying my downtime across Narragansett Bay in Newport.

"Well he says he's been with you for the past few weeks, has he?"

"Yes, he's been my crew since three weeks ago, we just got back from Lauderdale; we had a few weather delays."

I knew ZZ since he was in junior high school; his uncle is like an older brother to me, and ZZ and I had sailed together on his uncle's boat. ZZ knew that I had my own yacht delivery agency and that I was telling the truth. Apparently, as they were dragging Daedalus outside for his beating, he asked what for, and they told him that it was for having raped his ex-girlfriend.

An incredulous Daedalus retorted; "What the hell are talking about? When did she say I did this?"

They said "Last week."

He said "Well, I've been sailing on a boat for over three weeks, from Newport to Florida."

They said "With who?"

He said "With Captain Eric Wiberg."

At which point ZZ said "I know Eric, I'll call him."

He did call me, and I stuck up for my crew.

At which point a certain ex-girlfriend was taken aside, whether by men or women, for a talking to, and I don't think she had the alibi that Daedalus did. I hope they made her pay for his parking tickets! I didn't.

Part IV: Shoulders

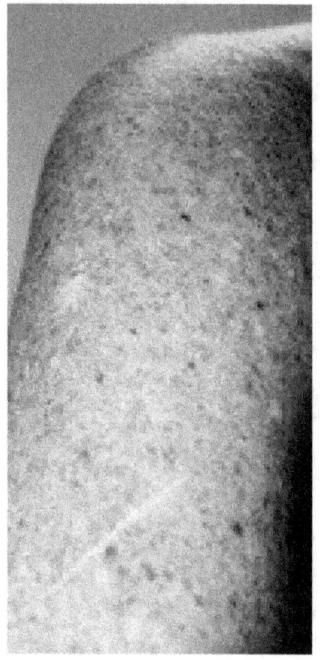

Photo: Right shoulder, from Cat Island, Bahamas metal scratch, 2019 and one of two cigarette burns, the lamp burn, 1986, which was later surgically excised and stitched.

Cat scratch:

    This is my favorite scar; ironically the lateral, three-inch prominent one on lower right arm was the most recent and innocuous! Compared with tiny ones a quarter inch long which have vastly more interesting back-stories. Fellow Swedes built a compound of several buildings at Port Royal, on the northwest tip of Cat Island, in the southeastern Bahamas. In 2019, my brothers and I brought our children, nieces, and nephews there by mailboat. It rained a lot, but we had a rented van for the group in which we explored the island, tip to tip, for a week. To keep food fresh and drinks cold we used a massive old white fishing cooler from my brother's boat.

  The hinges on the cooler lid – it was about 4 feet long and 2 feet deep – had worn free ages ago. That left them sticking out, sharp bits of twisted metal. With so many of us piling in and out of the car and my brother, more local than I, driving, I slid into the passenger seat one day, and as I did so my right arm conveniently scraped one long time against the metal, leaving only a very superficial, shallow wound, a thin seam of blood, and to my delight, a highly visibly and photogenic scar!

  I've often joked that the middle child likes to have maximum credit for minimum exertion; my siblings would wash the dishes, I would merely dry and fuss around, but as soon as they were done I would crow for credit! This little scar was a silly accident which resulted in a snazzy scar. That's how it works sometimes, I guess! It's so good that I didn't even have to make up a story about it; it's *cooler* than that!

Both of the cigarette burns are covered in *Part I: Shame Scars*, *Part VI: Self-harm*, and *Part VII: Surgeries*. One of them had three steps; a lamp burn in 1986, a cigarette burn in 1988 (also at St. George's), and then, after 2006, the scars from having it surgically excised and stitched.

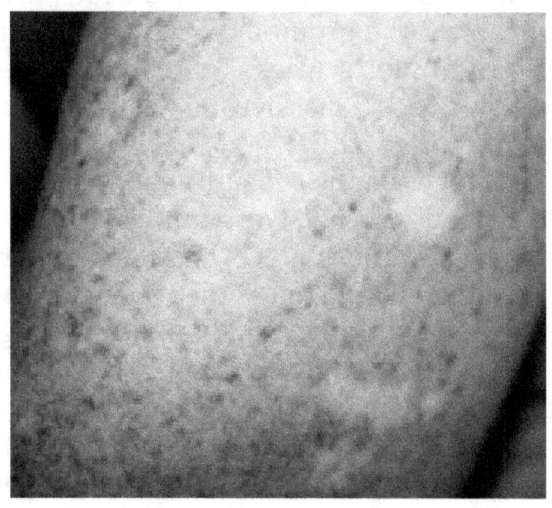

Photo: Surgery on top of shoulder, to repair, remove cigarette burn, outer upper left arm.

The lower right scar going sideways across the arm was from operating a small boat in Singapore – we were on the way to Turtle Island in a friend's small speedboat and went right over a flat of shoals. I hopped out to push us clear and in doing caught my shoulder on a sharp clevis pin or similar, which seemed very innocuous at the time but turned into a shallow, wide scar.

Note that, being born in 1970 in New York City, I did not receive vaccinations to any upper arm, so all these scars were from later in life. All of the cigarette burns are on the right side of my body, as I smoke with my left and so it was always a lot easier to distinguish them on the opposite side; it gave me more accuracy and control.

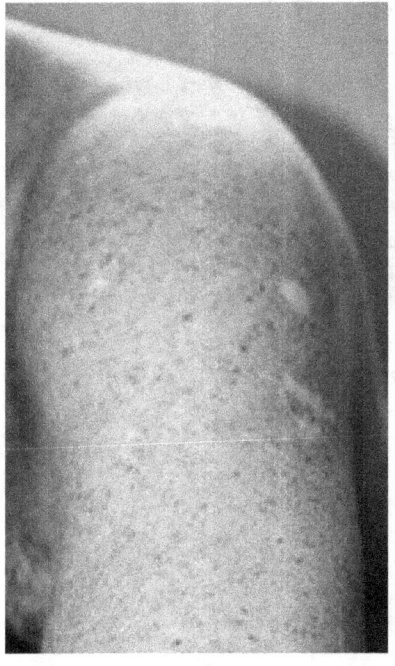

Photo: Left shoulder: various surgeries upper left outer shoulder, left arm.

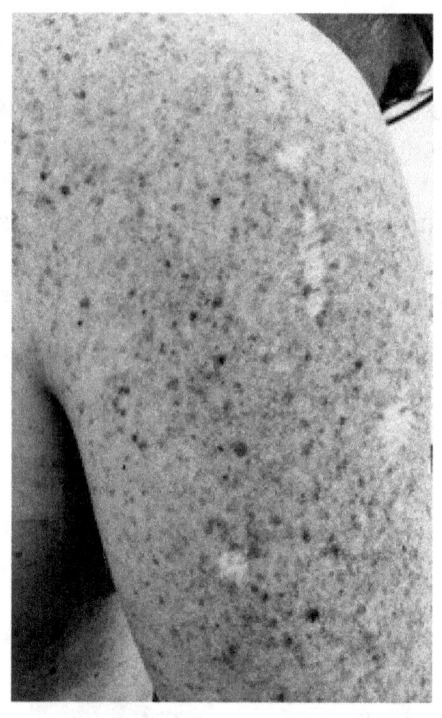

Photo: Various surgeries to upper left, outer shoulder, left arm.

Part V: Torso, front & back

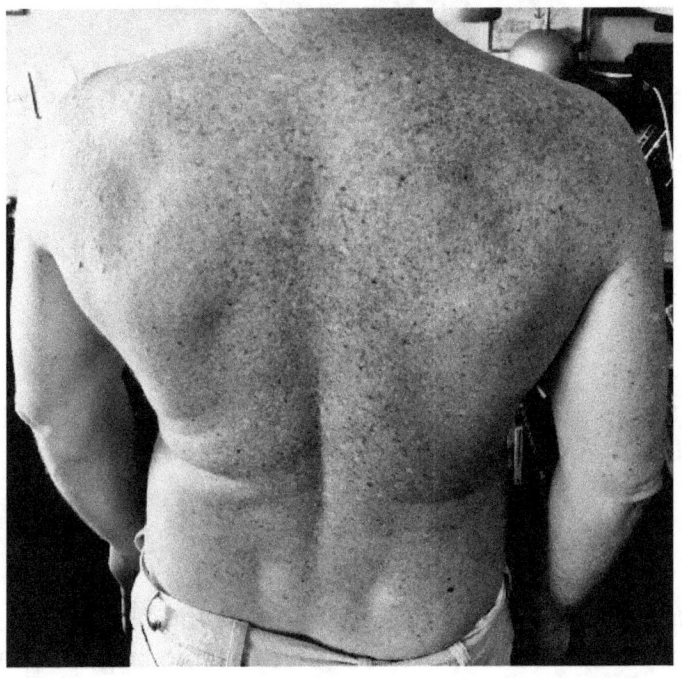

Photo: Back; the white spots are remnants of *tinea versicolor* from swimming in Pape'ete Harbor, Tahiti, French Polynesia during my first job out of college skippering a boat to New Zealand. We were four Fridays in Pape'ete; I have the scars of flesh-eating bacteria to show it!

Photo: Given our Swedish citizenship and heritage, my three siblings and I worked on the same large hunting and farming estate in southeastern Sweden, each for a different summer. The poor famers assumed each child might remotely resemble the previous, as in "we know you love ketchup, so we bought a lot!" and were often disappointed that we did not.

I arrived late with really no farming experience, and at age 17 was immediately left behind by the farmers who went on holiday. I had about three days of training. The sun didn't set and it was an extraordinary and inspired six weeks or so, with only a bit of drama (or human interaction). This photo was taken by Lars, the lead employed farmer, who was saving up money to pay for his 17-year-old daughter to have scars from an earlier surgery removed.

Grazed by crazed bull: Diary; July 16, 1987:

"I have been living on Edeby farm alone for three nights now. I run the whole farm and estate. Both mornings have had great unusualities: on Wednesday morning (yesterday) I went to feed the bulls. When I got to the single-cow cell of an expecting mother, I was surprised, for I caught out of the corner of my eye, a second cow. It turns out to be a tiny calf and fresh in its birth-blood, yet completely dead. Flies buzzed around its large, round eyes and the mother ate tiredly. I was the only one here, so I called up one of Han's friends and we threw the corpse into the back of a butcher truck.

This morning when I went to feed the bulls, I found bullshit where it shouldn't have been. Then I made the worrying realization that one of the bulls was sodomizing his chained-up companions, and goring them with large horns. Like a fool, I imitated the wizened old farmer, and stood in the recalcitrant bull's path, arms akimbo, and ordered him into an open stall. I was honestly expecting him to timidly obey, as, after the previous day's drama, I was in no mood for his gay acts.

Instead of entering the stall, he came at me with his head down, shaking his horns. He came so slowly that I thought he would not touch me. Besides, I thought that I was in control. I was wrong on both counts. He swung his head three times, and on the third he grazed my stomach, and his horn ripped through my T-shirt and left just a smidgen of blood. Even though this incident didn't leave a scar, it scared the fuck out of me. I ran to and clawed my way up and over a set of tall steel stall railings to escape and landed safely in a locked pen. Jesus, so close! After that I just cunningly left certain gates open, to create a maze in which his antics would be contained and he could not rape nor swipe, and I could feed and water him until help arrived.

I wrote a short, fun poem commemorating this experience, and read it to the St. George's School Poetry Club, which I co-founded with L.A. surfboard-maker Alex Kemp:

Poem: Death Row:

> I live on death row,
> And so do you.
> Just like the cows do –
> We all do: *Moooo!*

Note: this is not a Haiku, which is only 3 lines, each with 5, then 7, then 5 syllables."

Skin infections from swimming in Pape'ete Harbor:

Photos: Views of Pape'ete Harbor, Tahiti, Polynesia, showing the Scottish-registered 68-foot yacht

Stornoway, with red ensign, which at age 23 was under my command, *en route* to New Zealand. When a neighbor's yacht's anchors got all tangled in the mess of lines in the languid harbor with many live-aboards, I foolishly leapt in to help clear the mess, catching a years-long skin infection from the fetid water, into which lots of rotten food from vendors, and who knows what else, rats and effluent, flowed.

From memoir *Round the World in the Wrong Season*:

"The watershed or geographical tipping point of our voyage (Tahiti) behind us, we faced the final leg of our saga. It was as though the rot which seemed to swell in the dingy lanes of the city had tried to hold us back, in the clutches of failure and abandonment which had been the undoing of others before, and doubtlessly since. *Stornoway* had grown a beard of marine fungi and weeds around her waterline, and barnacles had seized up her spinning wheel.

This isn't surprising, given that for years afterwards I suffered from odd white patches of skin missing from my chest, back, and arms that the dermatologist labeled *tinea versicolor*. I trace this back to my swims in Tahiti's filthy harbor – to the effluent, city runoff and food-stall refuse pouring into it."

Diary; October 28, 1994:

"In the kitchen, my Farmor's flat, Karlavägen 50, Östermalm, Stockholm. ...My new address is *Danderyd's Sjukhus*, which stands for *sick house*, or hospital in the suburb of Danderyd. Farmor took me here urgently in a taxi when I had infectious breakouts...., *tinea versicolor* on my chest and back from swimming in crappy water in Pape'ete, and quite severe fevers.

I'm in room 15, ward 96, which is for infectious diseases just outside Stockholm, Sweden. I'm not supposed to leave, but I get out on a roof-like balcony where other inmates smoke, but we don't speak to each other. I am not supposed to have guests, but Stefan (the sailor I hired in Tonga to sail to New Zealand months before) came by with a suitcase of whisky, Carlsberg beer and cigarettes, which we consumed in the hospital room....."

Surgeries to torso and back:

Several surgical removals from chest, and back, and at least one from belly. Also the upper right birthmark was self-removed for swimming, using the scissors on a Swiss army knife, and one or two have been removed from upper chest.

Photo: Scar from surgery to back, upper left shoulder.

Part VI: Legs, buttocks to feet

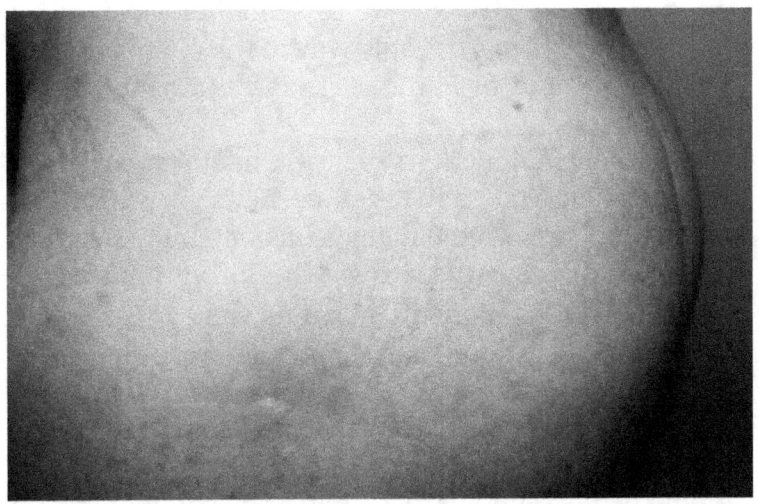

Photo: Left buttock, outside, from jeans snagging a bolt on Martin (Pinzón's) boat Ambassador Beach Hotel c.1984.

Mate to Captain Pinzón:

One of the larger-than-life characters growing up on an island in the Bahamas with more than its share of tax-exiles, expatriates, Bahamians whose home islands are redolent with culture and who in the early 1970s were claiming their independence, was Martin T., aka Pinzón. He was nicknamed after Martín Alonso Pinzón was captain of the *Pinta*, one of the original three Columbus ships to land in the Bahamas in 1492; he and his brother went on to be renown sailors and navigators in that era. For starters, Martin and his brother Brock rode to school every day in a boat, because it was the only way to the mainland from the western end of Paradise Island that their family lived on.

Their father was a sea captain and so is Randy, their brother in law, and together they took passengers on long cruises of the Bahamas on a medium-sized tall ship. One of their guests was the heavy metal band AC⚡DC who like many other bands were recording at Compass Point Studios nearby, which was founded by Jamaican producer who helped promote Bob Marley, Chris Blackwell. Well, even though I first met Pinzón when he chased me up a tree and dared me to come down to the schoolyard to get an ass-whooping for being mean to a smaller child, we became friends over the years, and I looked up to him – literally, as he was over a year older and about two feet taller! He had the calm demeaner and blonde good looks of Sterling Hayden, known for the films *Bahama Passage* and the crazy air force general in *Dr. Strangelove*, and for his books *Wanderer* and *Voyage*.

I remember I had my first real "drunk" at Martin's island getaway home astride both sides of Paradise Island. Hanging out with him at his place was really cool. My other good friend, Frank, was the son of scientist and an only child who went on to be a marine biologist. While with both Frank and Martin I was able to gain maritime exposure, only with Pinzón was there the added thrill of alcohol and possibly even girls! At that point I was only 12 or so, as by my 13th birthday I left essentially for good.

On the night in question Pinzón had talked two teenage girls, at Club Med, whose beach was adjacent to his home, known for its topless sunbathing, promiscuity, and as a place where local boys could work in the aquasports side for a summer or two and have so much sex with guests and staff that they might actually tire out! Pinzón and I set out from his dock on a Boston Whaler-type open outboard motor boat about 17 feet long. In calm harbor conditions met the girls at the Club Med dock, less than a mile away, after dinner.

We took them west through Nassau Harbour, between Arawak Cay and Crystal Cay, to the wide bay which makes Cable Beach, where I grew up. On the eastern end of the beach, in Goodmans' Bay, we anchored facing the open water, and backed down to the beach, enabling the girls to disembark relatively drily on the beach. To be honest, it was probably the first time I handled a boat at night, and instead of the Khaki shorts Pinzón had on, I was wearing cumbersome jeans. I had to jump off to secure the boat, and somehow my left butt-cheek caught on a metal screw on the hand-rail, ripping my jeans, causing me to bleed, and hurting like hell!

Well, of course with the end-game in sight of kissing one of the girls, I bit my tongue and said nothing. We went to the Ambassador Beach Hotel, which then operated the Playboy Casino, which not only featured women dressed in bunny outfits, allowed free alcohol drinks and constant cigarette smoking, but also allowed us kids free reign! (I had grown up bilking the slot machines, but that's another story).

After an hour or so, Pinzón suggested we pop over to a nearby island. We re-boarded, I pulled up the anchor and we motored less than a mile north to lovely, uninhabited Long Cay. This islet, now owned by the same music producer Chris Blackwell, is shaped like the profile of a whale, and where the fins would be, is a small rectangular beach jutting into Delaport Bay, perfectly small so that if you are there on a boat, no one else would deign to join and bother you.

We anchored again, this time without much fuss, as the beach was sheltered and the breeze was offshore. Once ashore, we made a small fire of driftwood and shared rum and cokes in cups which the experienced captain had brought. Then I understood the night's strategy, as devised by Pinzón and the older girl of the two; one of them was "hot to trot" with the good captain, the other one was much more contemplative and disdainful of the pleasures of the flesh. Of course that meant Miss well-behaved would be my date, and that it was my duty to enjoy (or endure) the other, younger girls' company while Pinzón and her friend got it on in the dunes, as it were. So endure I did.

Whether because she learned I was going to boarding school in Massachusetts in the fall or independently, she launched into the saga of how her father was a scholarship student at Philips Andover prep school, had then gone on to make a good living for himself and the couple were raising two daughters. But when it came to sending them to boarding school, he made the moral stand that either his daughters obtained scholarships to Philips Andover as well, or they could damn-well go to public school, as he had at first, too!

So off to public school this clearly disappointed, betrayed, unhappy girl made sure I knew. I would say that my interested in her wilted, but it was never given the oxygen to develop. I literally had a pain in my ass while spending two windy hours listening to another pain in the ass, all so that my friend Pinzón could get a piece of ass.

Then we went back by boat. I almost recall having to find their condom on the beach, but that's probably an embellishment. I do have the scar to remind me of the evening. It was, to use the turn Walter Lord's nautical phrase, a night to remember, yet perhaps better forgotten.

Impetigo:

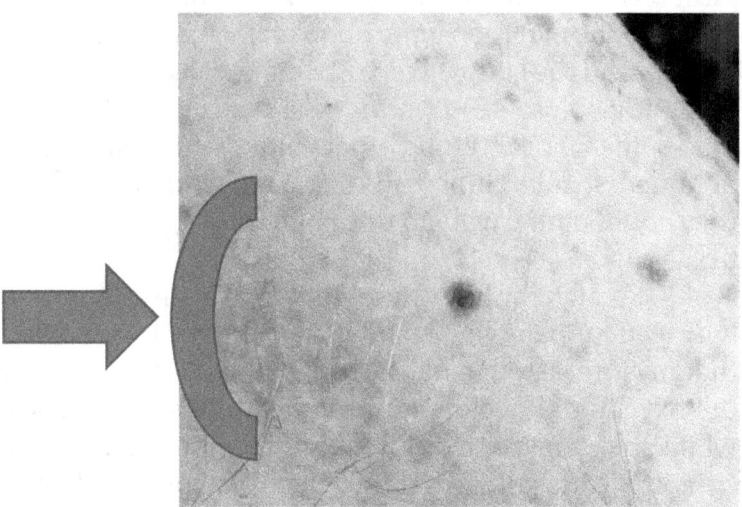

Photo: At the left of the black freckle is the outline of a circle; the black spot it towards the upper-right time. Though barely visible after 45 years, there is an inch-wide scar on the inside of my left arm left by a very painful and deep Impetigo infection which drove my mother to distraction. And five-year-old-me as well!

Kid's Stuff:

While young (age six or so) I had bad cases of impetigo, or deep infections from staph and strep my on left buttock and inner, upper left arm. The problem with impetigo is that most of us aren't familiar with it, and though in appearance it can be small, in reality the infection can run rather deep and be not only painful but last many days, even weeks. From my recollection, even lancing them didn't banish the infection. Not much fun! But at least it left scars, which chicken pox did not.

The Mayo Clinic says this about impetigo: "It is usually caused by staphylococcal (staph) bacteria, but it can also be caused by streptococcal (strep) bacteria. It is most common in children between the ages of two and six. ....A more serious form of impetigo, called ecthyma, penetrates deeper into the skin, causing painful fluid, or pus-filled sores that turn into deep ulcers. The ulcers associated with ecthyma can leave scars." I had the ecthyma version; never more than two at a time, and as you can see, it left scars.

Cliff diving, Nassau, teens:

Photo: Above and below; our friend from L.A. and me horsing around while cliff diving during college. Since WWII Clifton Pier has been the commercial tanker ship dock for the capital's fuel supply. An unfinished jetty has easy access, height, and deep water, but the only way out is the jagged coral which with big waves presents a problem, resulting of course in scars. My brothers have dived there with Norwegian mountain climber and cliff diver Arne Næss accompanied by his wife, Diana Ross, and their children (Mr. Næss sadly died from a mountain climbing incident in South Africa; he felt it was better than golf!)

- Diary; March 15, 1988: " \\ // " on left leg, cliff-diving, waves dashed on rocks, 17.
- Diary; September 8, 1988: We went cliff diving at Clifton Pier, Nassau, Bahamas.

- Diary; April 18, 1989: In a few hours I give my one-and-only chapel talk, emphasizing individuality. Bleeding from leg (thorns) and hands (glass window broken last night) and reminded of cliff diving and rocky surf-induced blood.

Liberian Seamans Book, body identifiers:

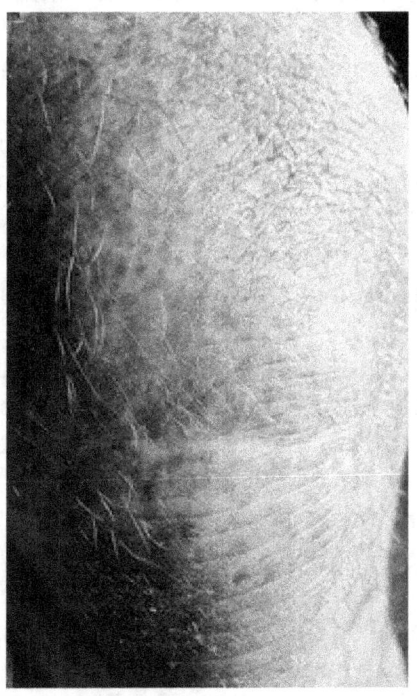

Photo: Scar across right knee cap, very slippery tennis court home, Nassau, 1978, Princes.

Butterflies are kneeded:

Not really so much to say about the scar across the knee; it wasn't for non-payment of debt, inflicted by a mobster in a back alley of Hell's Kitchen on Manhattan or the Combat Zone in Boston back in the 1980s'. Rather it was a tennis court mishap that wasn't either monitored or repaired properly.

I was about eight years old and my parents were away for the day. Usually this would mean "really" dangerous stuff like burning down the woods behind the house, finding human skulls with bullet hole in a pond, or a baby's skull in a plastic bag in the attic of a burnt out house, or sifting through the X-rated Polaroids of deadbeat tenants in the attic of the family apartments business (a story of its own, for the shrink), or having gang wars with the Irish kids in the vacant lot nearby. Or stealing golf balls and turtles from the nearby golf course, evading the security guard so that we could sell the loot to pet shops or teachers. Or climbing the abandoned water tower to take in the views, which consisted of iron ladders and walkways of which about 70% was wasted, and we didn't have cognitive skill to know which was safe…. And owls would often fly at our faces when disturbed.

Instead, on this particular day, we opted to have a fun, harmless game of softball on the family tennis court. It was the four of us, the King brothers, and a couple other neighbors – about eight altogether, without parental supervision, the oldest being perhaps eleven. I must have (uncharacteristically) actually hit the tennis ball with a stick, since I raced for home base, which is the center point where servers do their stuff. Whether I was tagged out or not, I don't recall, since I simply could not stop. I don't think I had shoes in the downpour, and the silky slippery surface of the court, with all that algae activated, meant I just went full speed into the rusty metal fence, which had no barrier.

The pain or risk of infection wasn't so bad, it was the wound and the blood, and having it mixed with rain made it seem like a lot more blood than there really was.

The neighborhood kids cooperative normally focused on peeping at the girls skinny-dipping, or arranging blankets and pillows for the junior ranks to watch the elders enjoying a wholesome outdoor viewing of the classic fuck-film *Caligula* (which says on the video box "appropriate for seven-year-olds," right?) Fortunately for me on that day the team really kicked in – either they called or ran down the street to get Mrs. Prince, British, who then took me to Dr. P., also British, who was the primary physician for most of the neighborhood, ably assisted by a kindly British or Guayanese woman of Indian descent; the Bahamas had been a British colony until half a decade earlier.

Dr. P.'s door was held open with a cannonball he found in Nassau Harbour with a SCUBA tank. He was so well known for his insouciance (of the "it's just a bug bite" variety from Monty Python) that it ultimately cost him his career. I don't remember the good doctor ever appearing young, but after a few decades of classic British stiff upper lips airiness ("you'll be right as rain," "nothing to worry about,") he told a patient with an rapidly failing heart that he was fine, only for the fellow to keel over of a stroke a short time later, leaving Dr. P. the option of returning to farming.

Well rather than stitch up my knee, he threw on some glorified Band Aids called "butterfly stitches," which combined with my active lifestyle and the absence of parenting or nursing, quickly fell off. Fortunately all of these well-meant failings in the healthcare system (except for Mrs. Prince the angel, who carried me to the arms of salvation), left me with a beautiful scar – I hope you agree!

The government of Liberia, who keep an office outside Washington DC, issued me a seafarer's license formally a "Seaman's Identification and Record Book" which prominently features my knee-cap scar, should my cadaver be found floating without other characteristics like teeth to identify me with. I shudder to think what scars were inflicted on innocents in Liberia's civil wars of the 1990s with those funds….

Photo: My first Liberian Seaman's Book, *Seaman's Identification and Record Book, Republic of Liberia* issued in 1995 on Duxton Hill in Singapore, enabling me to ride the company's dozen tankers, which I did to India and back shortly after my arrival. I was 25 and was at sea for a month, passing through the Andaman & Nicobar islands in the Bay of Bengal – a dream! And my, what a pretty maritime seal!

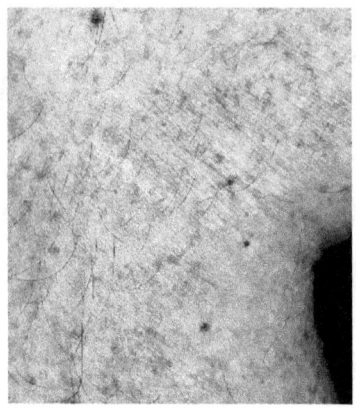

Photo: The skin nipped of by borrowed cleats from taking a pole vault high jump at St. Andrews, age 12. I really had no idea what I was doing, and never did that again.

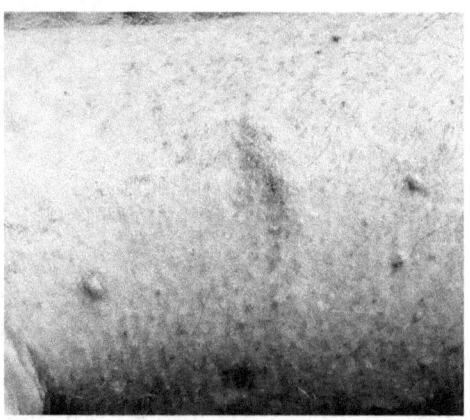

Photo: Dog bite, Doberman, while leaping into Ricky Z's pool, Nassau, Bahamas, aged 14, 1985.

Dang fang:

I looked up to Ricky and his brothers; they were from – and returned to – Abaco Island later. My intense interest in Ricky peaked around the time I was ratcheting up an attempt at seducing a girl a year older than me (age 15), and was due to leave on a sailboat named *Against the Wind*, after the Bob Seger song (I always felt: what a depressing name for a sailing boat). Ricky was my "alibi." The dog turned its naughty fangs on me during one of Ricky's birthday parties; he lived "out East" and we "out West." Although geographically only a few miles apart, the expatriate suburbs and the largely white Bahamian community were not always in sync socially, as bridging that gap meant drives through the capital and the potential discomfiture of either all-white or mixed clubs.

In any event, I was largely ignorant of all that when at age 11 or so I took a running leap into the Randall's pool, and their Doberman dog anticipated it, caught up with me, and, as you can see, made a well-timed, well-placed snap which connected with the inside of my knee. This caused a puncture wound which bulged out over time, but did not prevent me from indulging in the birthday cake and jocularity! And like most of my scars, made the event more memorable.

Lacerated leg examined by physician grandmother: Diary; August 19, 1991:

"It's 1:15 am. Stockholm, guest room, the big one overlooking, Karlavägen. Sitting in the patient examination room in my grandmother's private practice in Stockholm. A female doctor since the 1920's who ran a camp with 100,000 escapees from the Iron Curtain in Austria in the mid-1950s (she only lost one patient), she told me that a lacerated leg, from trying to jump a fence, my own height; 6 feet, ought to be stitched."

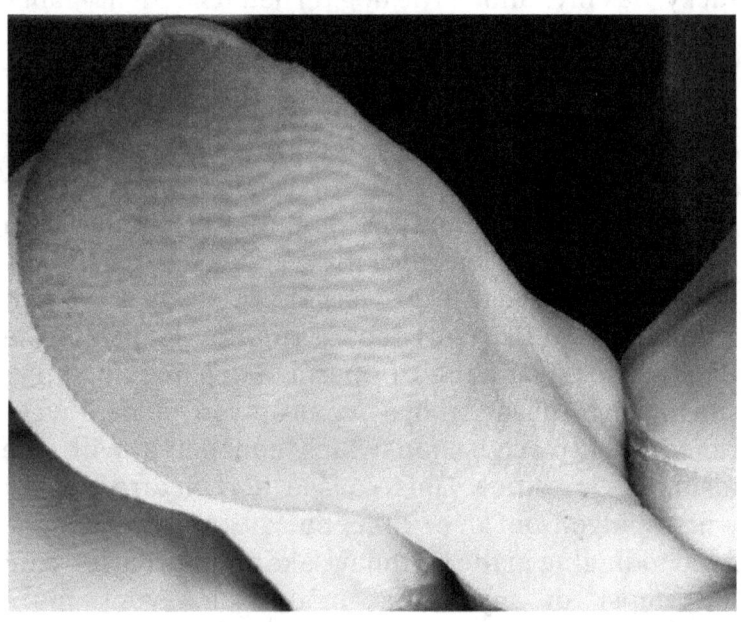

Photo: First toe in, from big toe, right foot. This one isn't actually much to look at... which is a good thing, as pretty much no one sees it.

Nearly de-toed: Diary; January 18, 1992:

"Warrington Hall Room 22, Harris Manchester College, Oxford, UK. Lo!, and behold; I changed the type of scissors, though with enough to have severely cut a toe years ago at St. George's (leading to heavy bleeding). Dave D. offered, pedophile F.C., choirmaster helped, Arden Dorm, Newport. That pretty much sums it up: my large left toenail was so resistant to conventional trimming (in the days before I lived in West Village, New York, and had paid pedicures with girlfriend as a matter of course) that I brought out the biggest guns I had, since I had no pliers.

A large set of art scissors would not do the trick either; I applied steady pressure on half the nail and it would not give. Then suddenly everything went sideways and askew, and the lower blade of the scissors jumped out of alignment with its cousin and cut through the lower bit of the next toe over (I'm left handed, so that would be on the right foot). At first I was not shocked, but damn if that thing didn't bleed like hell!

I literally hopped from my single room where I hobbled to the center of the hallway, collecting myself. Out of one of the known party rooms (every room but mine basically) came Dave D., who naturally offered to help when he saw all the blood. Not wanting to get the guys in trouble, I hopped down the hall, out into the vestibule, and knocked on teacher F.C.'s apartment; generally somewhere I had been trying to avoid since figuring out why there were personal portraits of dozens of students all over, particularly upstairs.

Any port in a storm, right? He patched me up well enough without sending me to old "Let's take a look down there" doctor who still lived with his mother, and I didn't have to do anything in exchange for the tourniquet and transfusion of a 50-gallon-drum of blood, so it was all good."

Cuts like a bike: Diary; June 26, 1993:

"Plymouth, New Hampshire: My last tetanus shot was in 1988 [since I cut my legs salvaging old bike *Cornelius* from Newport Harbor at Lee Wharf, I was sent by the Connetts to Dr. Wallace, the former St. George's School physician on Red Cross Lane]. The bike was so named as it's only identifier was a sticker from the City of Rye, New York, or C.O.R.N.Y., and my admiration for *Brideshead Revisited* by Evelyn Waugh (a World War II veteran, who *Time-Life Books* named one of the best *female* writers of the English language!), in which the main character has a Teddy bear named Aloysius: *Cornelius, Aloysius*; close enough!"

Photo: The Mitre Hotel, Singapore; driveway, front entry. We drowned the captured rats to the right, there were mango trees to the left. The big open window upper right on first photo was one of my rooms – the same window with colorful towel. Lee Kuan Yew, CGMG, the first independent leader of Singapore, lived around the corner, protected "only" by Gurkha guards, armed only with old Remington carbines and Kris's knives, which must be initiated by drawing blood, and once removed cannot be returned to the sheath having drawn blood. It is said (and more importantly believed) that if you insult or kill a Gurkha, they don't come after you directly, rather they start with your relatives....

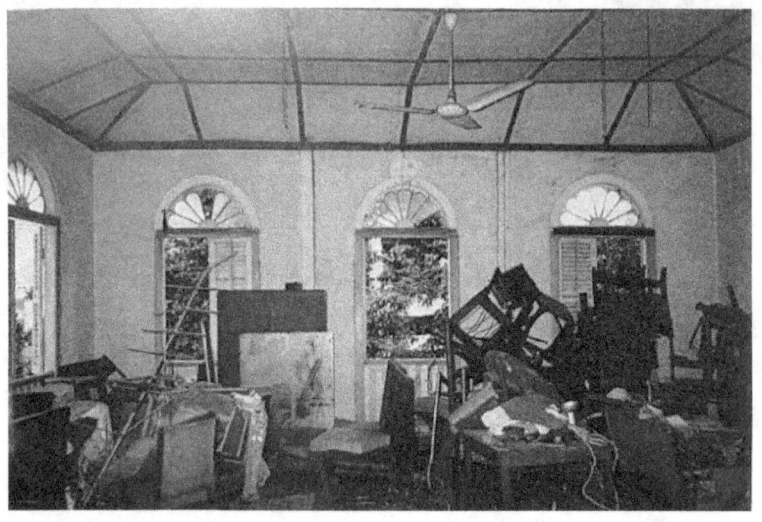

Photo: At some point this was the elegant reception or dining area, a common space in the Mitre Hotel in downtown Singapore. By 1996 and 1997, when I lived there, this area was a dumping ground for unwanted furniture, broken fans, and even many suitcases stuffed with personal belongings of tenants abandoned long ago. I once found four original British and Australian passports with photos of a man from his 20s to 50s who worked, as many who lived there did, in the commercial diving space.

Later, I was shocked to realize later that it was a fellow tenant I knew. He said when he boarded the plane for Singapore decades before, his dad had slipped him a large sum of cash; he interpreted that gesture as his father not wanting to see him again, when in fact it's more likely he was just being kind. But the man didn't return home because of the misunderstanding, and his original suitcase of a man full of promise embarking on a new career in a new region, is scattered like so much detritus, the man a habitué of the bar.

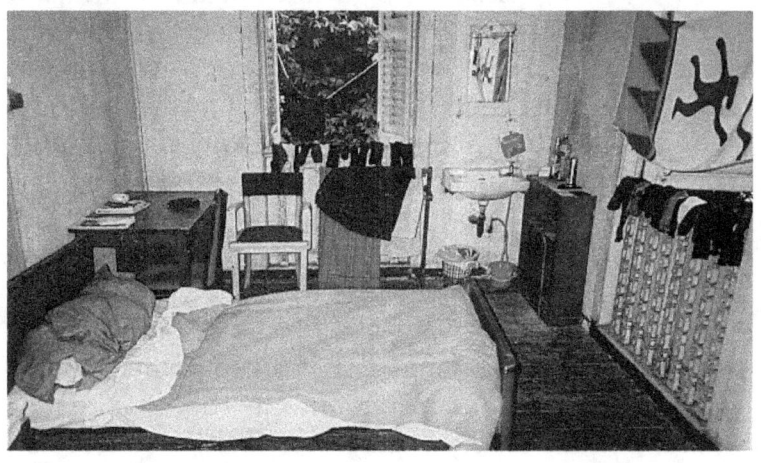

Photo: The infamous grandfathered ruin known as Mitre Hotel on Killeney Road, downtown Singapore, a block from fancy Orchard Road.

I'm not a fan:

In my mid-20s I lived in the notoriously downtrodden late-night watering hole named the Mitre Hotel. Set atop a priceless bit of commercial realty, nevertheless, due to a combination of Japanese occupiers having massacred young Chinese on the premises and multiple members of the same family failing to come to terms and sell it, it just deteriorated, with empty bottles and newspapers going back literally decades.

My occupancy, while I operated tankers from 1995 to 1998, lasted for eight memorable months. It was brought about by what I considered a series of expensive betrayals by landlords and roommates playing footloose and free with my deposits, my rent, and even my Australian girlfriend (I worked very late). The hotel's unusual tariff was 31 Singapore dollars per night, but if they saw me entertain and host a guest, 33! About USD$1.50 per guest per night. For furniture I scavenged from the hallways, the water was all cold, there was no shower curtain, I had two small turtles and numerous free-range rats for roommates (when they leapt out of the ceiling onto my bed one night I found a more sanitary place to live; yet one could hardly find a more memorable one! Everything from people to piss was also known to fall through the ceiling.

It was a strange place, where a young Brooklyn loner accused a one-eyed Swedish alcoholic known as Popeye of sleeping with my Swedish grandmother. He had to be dragged outside for his own safety; to protect him from me and the regulars. For years he had sat there, listening to the drunk eccentrics, taking notes for god-knows-what novel, not revealing anything about himself. But after a conversational sucker-punch against Popeye and my beloved Farmor, he never came back. An etching of a black cat with arched back, symbolizing a Scottish Highlander regiment which was the last across the causeway from Johor Bahru prior to the fall of Singapore in World War Two, still remains.

One night I watched as elderly Japanese men and younger family members sat whispering in a corner, occasionally, pointing to all the places they were when they lived in the building during the Japanese occupation, which lasted for so many years that they renamed Singapore *Syonan*, and the *Kempeitai* secret police barracks produced so many horrific screams into the night that residents of the area of what is now the Shaw's theater had trouble sleeping – even after the Japanese left. I remember late one night the Malay and other older vendors at the Newton Circus food court suddenly tensed up; I immediately looked around to find out why, and saw a freshly arrived tour bus was discharging much older Japanese tourists.... The old time Singaporeans were alive then tens of thousands of their young men were massacred. You could feel the tension and visceral, involuntary discomfort, but the Japanese apparently did not.

A whisky bottle of chilled water waited outside my door before work each day. If I went "sober" and stayed away from the bar too many days, meaning they made less money off of me, the "dose" of whiskey left at the bottom of the cold water would increase. I noticed this, as I would grab the cold bottle of water each morning before work and gulp down the contents. If I didn't slow down, a quarter-shot of Whiskey would make it into my throat!

If gradually sneaking more Whisky into my body daily didn't work, there was an Indian loan-shark who drove a brand-new white Mercedes Benz and parked it in front of the bar. My made me explain that on February 1st each year I liked to go sober off cigarettes, booze, or both, and that I had never made it past Valentine's Day. I'm not sure what was in it for him, but he then gave me his intelligence file on me; where I worked, what building, who my colleagues were, what my employer did, and my specific role. He said that his inquiries were satisfactory, and that I was held in sufficiently good esteem by the locals he spoke with. Then he handed me an Anchor beer in a cold can, and I drank it.

In a very conservative city the bar tender was a butch lesbian, the old man was revered by all as "Uncle," I met everyone from a Shakespearean troupe to a former phone-sex worker from New York City who was of a darker hue, officially a lesbian, but came up to Singapore from Indonesia on visa runs and was known to dabble one the junkets. One night some European acquaintances banged on my door for me to adjudicate between them and Uncle. Turns out they were smoking pot in the attic and fallen into one of the rooms, and he was demanding they either pay the repairs off or fix it themselves. I turned to Uncle and said "throw the book at them!" They were dismayed at my betrayal of racial allegiance. But they had disregarded my home and my landlord in dangerous ways.

A skinny British junky with a Thai girlfriend crashed out of his window flying on heroin, but survived, injured. After I left a man of Indian descent died, apparently of heart attack, at the stop of the stairwell and was there a couple days and *rigor mortis* by the time he was removed. I'm told a large party I threw there advertised by Cambodian boat-child-turned soya and palm-oil business success Michael M., was the first party in Singapore promoted using a new technology called electronic mail, or email....

Downstairs lived Thai (front) and Filipina (back) prostitutes, and upstairs men, mostly western, and mostly South African commercial divers, and British. My injury took place in the middle photograph above; the public area where detritus like the broken fan was left. By way of background, the Thai women lived downstairs. We hardly ever saw them, it was like a dorm or barracks, where they slept in the day and used a steam cooker for rice and mostly padded around in cheap plastic sandals in unsexy casual wear, hear in curlers and swearing at each other in a language few of us understood.

One of the "girls" (she might have been in her 30s or 40s for all we knew), had bought some CDs to play music with, but never had her own CD-player to listen to the music on. Her *nom-de-guerre* was Apple, since most of her clients would have butchered her real, Thai name. I suspect there was a CD player in their dorm, but there were fights over who could play what, and no headphones.

From her perspective, I was known as a steady tenant who went to the office every day, didn't do drugs, and wasn't cruel to anyone. Pretty much there was a low bar for decency at the place. I also moved rooms about four times until I found my palace; a large main room, many closets, airy bureau in front of a forested window to set my turtles atop, a bathroom with bath and large windows, and some plush faux leather couches and tables. I also had been given large nautical flags, salvaged from a sunken ship in the Malacca Straits by South African divers, and I hung these gaily in the ceiling tiles above the entire main room. It was a festive, airy, breezy, private space.

I also had a CD player. So Apple, one of the few Thai girls who interacted with the staff of the hotel (Uncle and his niece), approached me to see if I needed a hand cleaning my apartment? I told her I would gladly accept – the hotel was spotty at best at cleaning and I preferred to buy my own sheets and do it myself. Which meant that the floor had not been swept or mopped for weeks. I didn't have much valuable in the room, but it was all my possessions in the world during three years Out East, so I preferred she clean the place on weekends, when I was there. All she asked was the privilege of playing her CDs on my CD player, which was great by me!

The only caveat was that of course I was not to hover or interrupt her. She would basically do the cleaning naked, dancing around the room with a mop and broom, and I let her at it. Never of course, mixed business with pleasure. But I had to amble around the property for a couple of hours or run errands until Apple was done, which we all knew because suddenly the Thai pop music would cut off.

I was also barefoot moping around upstairs, looking at all the crap piled up in the waiting area and not paying enough attention. A round circular aluminum fan was lying on the floor and tilted at just such an angle that as I moved my foot forward, not seeing it, the top of my foot was cut by the outer edge, drawing blood, and creating a three-inch-or-so cut there. Well, it stung and hurt but was more visual than painful.

When Apple came out soon afterwards and noticed the blood on my foot, she instinctively grabbed a bottle of Whiskey (he had no language in common), and doused and dabbed the wound with it, ensuring it would become a scar. Then she got some dressings and bandages from the bar and kindly dressed my cut. Apple proved herself a sweet person who was giving and caring. So far as I remember, she only cleaned my place twice, maybe thrice, before her work or health took her away from Singapore, she perhaps made enough for her own CD player, or went back to Thailand. As for me, I eventually couldn't handle the rats, which forced me more than once to walk miles to the office at 4 am or 5 am to avoid them, and I moved out.

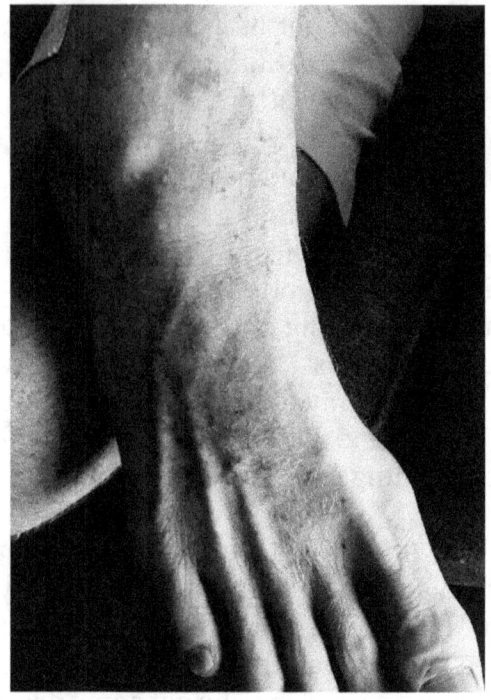

Photo: Top of right foot, detail, scraped base of junked ceiling fan, while Apple cleaned my room, and then the wound at the Mitre Hotel.

Note: It was *not* a brothel (really); our housemates lived and did not work there. However, I did hear Dragon Lady (one of the senior Filipina sex workers) ask a tenant if he had been filming, and heard another story of a check being slid under a door as compensation; prostitution is legal in Singapore, it is pimping which is outlawed.

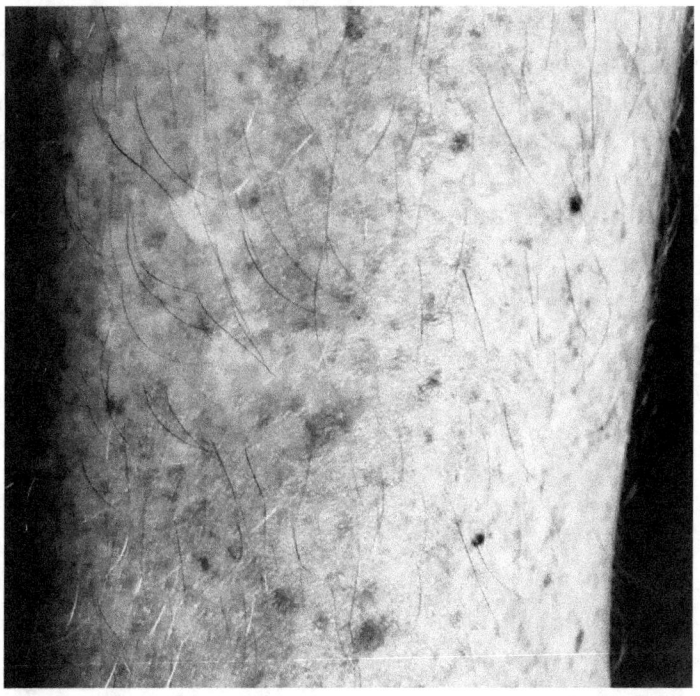

Photo: Instep or right leg, "branded" letter V for VMJ-C, then in Ireland, I was at Oxford, early 1991. Right front heel, inside leg, swinging backpack with Kevin S. at Eaglebrook. The ballpoint ink branded me, about age 13, first year of boarding school, 1984.

What brand is that can opener?: Diary; March 5, 1992:

"Oxford, UK. S. D, my US roommate, & V. M. J.-C were in Ireland together at the same time I was writing to them (he was supposed to be in Spain). I also branded my lower right inner ankle with a *V* for V. using a can opener shaped like a *U* or a *V* at that same time in my Warrington room; later S. developed a close friendship with my senior year girlfriend while I was off sailing! All innocent…"

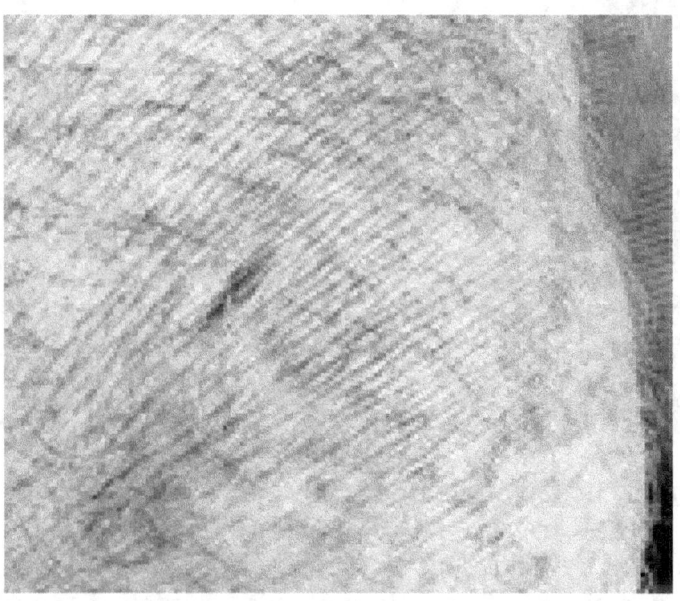

Photo: Right knee cap, showing where metal stained the skin due to rust from Tongan Japanese *Maru* fishing vessel April, 1994.

Photo: The actual Japanese long-lining fishing vessel in TongaTapu, Nuku'Alofa, Tonga.

Stop needling me:

From *Round the World in the Wrong Season*, memoir of crossing the South Pacific in command of the 68-foot yacht *Stornoway*, between Panama in December, 1993 and Auckland, New Zealand, in May, 1994;

After this exhausting night I set out to walk along the coast away from development. I followed the main coastal road to the east, past a small naval base with Swedish-built patrol vessels flying the Tongan flag which looked remarkably like the Swiss. It quickly became an unpaved track leading to miles of coconut groves and an old quarry. My ability to tour being limited by my budget, I set off in the rain with my foul weather coat on, but when the rain stopped the heat was oppressive.

When a rain squall suddenly hit, I ran for the shelter of a coconut grove. Steaming from the waterproof jacket, I fell asleep under the tree. Hours later a local farmer spotted me and I spotted him scurrying in the opposite direction. For weeks I was known by the locals as the *Palangi ko hai 'oku mohe 'i ha lalo 'akau*, or *foreigner who sleeps under the tree*. I am glad that I didn't have a customary wank out there, as evidently my every move had been watched by locals with rapt curiosity.

On another occasion I walked to a shipwrecked Japanese tuna-fishing boat at low tide. From the top of the bridge I became mesmerized by the darting fish, and recalled the many nights my childhood friend Frank and I would devote to catching just a few of them. I started flinging rust scales at the lightning-fast needle fish. From such a height they could not anticipate the projectiles, and with a deep arsenal I soon wounded one of them.

In my rush to retrieve its corpse three decks below, I fell forward, lost my balance, hit the rusty old bulkhead, and cut my knee. Though the wound itself was slight, a sliver of flaking, rusted iron embedded in my skin. To get the chips out and avoid tetanus, I used the needle nose of the fish to extract some (but not all) of the metal. As you can see, a small piece still lies in my kneecap, reminding me of the odd episode.

Part VII: Self-scarring

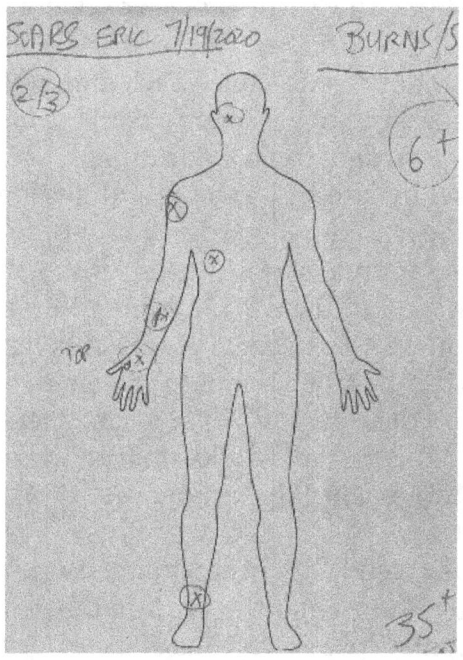

Photo: Etching by author of self-inflicted cigarette burns and other cutting scars.

Don't put that out!:

Excerpt from a report submitted to the Rhode Island State Police investigating St. George's School's decades of abuse of some estimated 100 (or more) victims.

"People have been interested in why I put cigarettes out on myself. The first time took place in Vietnam, or Korea - the names we used for the thick bushes behind the gym and several dorms on the western edge of campus. There was an old wooden outdoor paddle tennis court back there where girls would sunbathe - boys would watch from the clock tower above Arden–Diman dormitory. None of these places exist anymore - they are buildings, fields.

It began innocuously enough - I had a bothersome anomaly on the skin of my upper right arm, and I tried to burn it off. I ended up putting the cigarette out on it. I am convinced that I was punishing my body for betraying me to Coleman. If he was attracted to the "beauty" of my body then I would disfigure it and no one would want to harm me going forward. Adolescent logic, I now realize, but I was an adolescent.

Years later a dermatologist, perhaps not surprisingly, found that the burn had become a Basal cell carcinoma - pre-cancerous - and had it removed, requiring nine stitches. The other burns were inflicted while I was in college in Boston - to the ankle (while in Oxford), the face (Boston) and two to the hand (Newport). For the most part they have healed nicely."

Right inside forearm, half of beer can, getting drunk with RTW prior to a late-night rugby practice, which proved to be my last at Boston College, as I was unfit for the sport. This scar was later diagnosed as Basal cell and surgically removed. Later, a cigarette burn on the left top of right hand, by self, during a tumultuous freshman year of college."

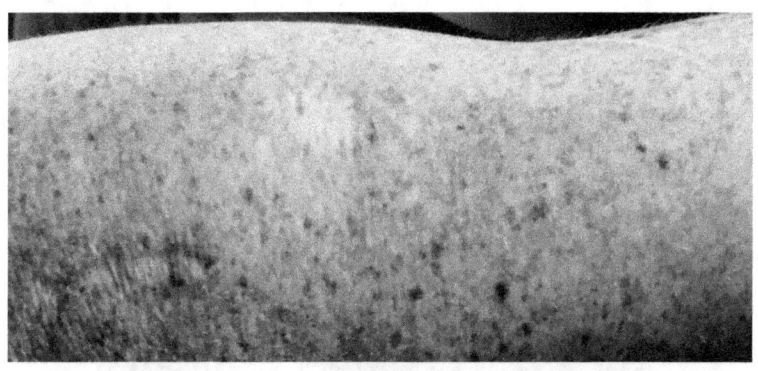

Photo: Three wounds to upper right shoulder from behind: Left, a surgery from sun damage, middle the burn from a lamp, then a cigarette, then surgery and third, in upper right, the Cat Island scratch.

"Time take a cigarette, puts it in your mouth...."
David Bowie; *Rock n' Roll Suicide*

Right cheek; this took place on Crosby Road, virtually on Boston College's campus, in the linoleum-lined kitchen of my girlfriend Natasha, her girlfriend Nancy (yes), and my good friend R. T. W.. I was quite lit, and when Nancy intervened to defend Natasha I quietly put the lit cigarette out on my face to show contrition and draw positive attention to myself – it was in fact rather nauseating for all involved. Then

burns to upper right shoulder (later surgery), middle right shoulder, outer right hand, inner right hand.

Photo: Nancy and I. We shared the same workplace; Murray's Liquors in Newton Center, and the same girlfriend, Natasha. We, however, did not date; only did things like this non-stop drive from Boston to Washington, D.C. and back in a colleague's borrowed car in the winter of 1989-1990. Later, Nancy was dismissed from Boston College after (allegedly) assaulting two campus policemen. I had seen her assault men before, and find the allegation creditable; for the record, I recommend against tangling with Nancy!

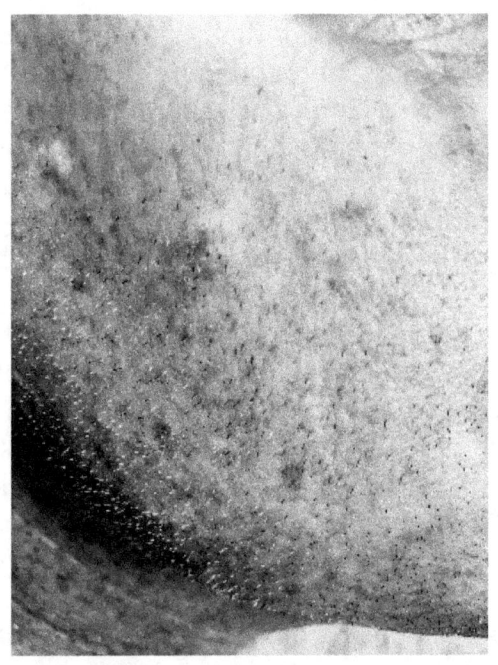

Photo: Right cheek, showing both sun damage and, a center-upper-left, the whiter-colored scar left from a self-inflicted cigarette burn on Crosby Street, near Boston College, fall of Freshman year, after being yelled at by the woman who was concurrently sleeping with my girlfriend.

Un-swimmable:

    I cut off two birthmarks, on right stomach, the other under right arm for swimming. The first got me evicted from my Sophomore year dorm at St. George's.

I returned from a football game against Tabor Academy to find my stuff in the hall, and was approached by a Smurf of a student proctor that I wasn't "good enough material" for the school. Turned out I was happier writing in my own room, but it was a confusing episode.

My roommate, who orchestrated it, was in the first two weeks of his family's boarding school experience, and due to not playing any sport the first season, he had time to play the proctor like a Machiavellian minion. Admittedly, I had left a bleeding handkerchief with the bit of flesh on my desk, which I understand could be quite unsettling to a kid fresh from the 'burbs in the mid-west, or to anyone. I should be grateful that the matter never escalated beyond just "kids."

Fact is that the dorm masters, or adults at that time barely showed their faces all year, leaving discipline and even room changes to 17-year-old, pimple-faced dorm prefects; to say that the job of living with and administering boys from 14 to 16 years old went to willing sadists would be an understatement, and barely scratches the surface of the cruelties, sexual and others, enacted in the 1980s at St. George's and other boarding schools, in the bathrooms, showers, faculty bedrooms, hallways, garbage barrels, basements, and quadrangles. That's a story for another day.

For arms:

Cut right forearm twice; first with my younger brother Nassau, sitting in the family living room, just so I could show what I was able and willing to do to myself. I was about 19 in college, he 17 and in boarding school. Second the drunken workup with my friend R. T. W. towards my last rugby practice in Newton, Massachusetts during our freshman year.

I remember turning the lights out and filling the metal ashtray with rubbing alcohol and lighting it for ambience. Predictably, this was not a brilliant idea, as we tipped over the ashtray, and the burning rubbing alcohol spilled onto my school back-back, an old cotton army-navy sack which caught fire with my books in it. We put the fire out with water, and beer, but my books were wet and singed, and the backpack smelled very richly of fire (and beer – the rubbing alcohol wore off), when I carried into buses and classes for the remaining months.

Photo: Right forearm, showing where while getting lit before winter rugby practice in college I scraped my arm with half a crushed beer can.

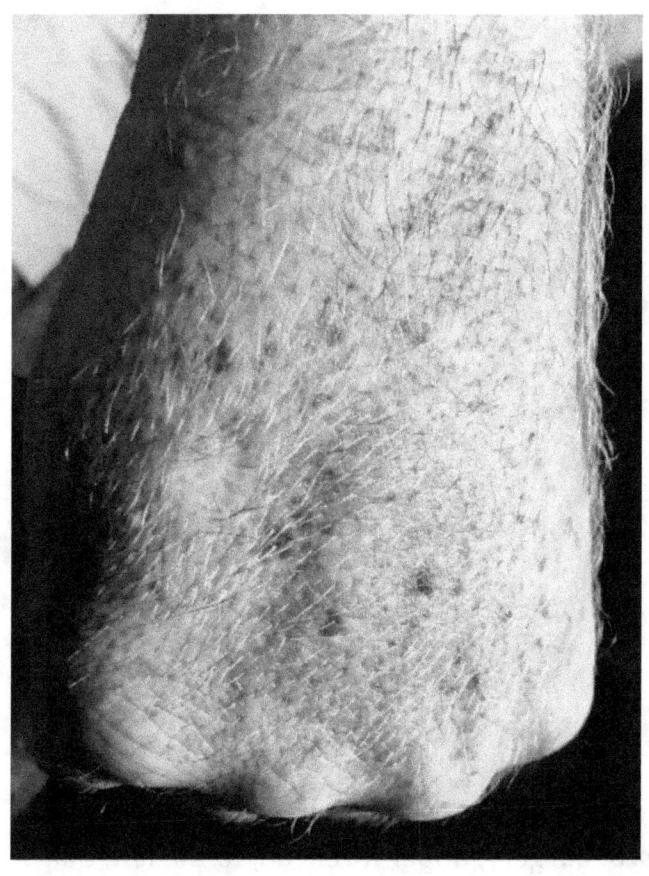

Photo: The "Bermuda-Race" cigarette burn to the outside of my right hand is visible above the fourth knuckle from the right in this photo.

Part VIII: Surgeries

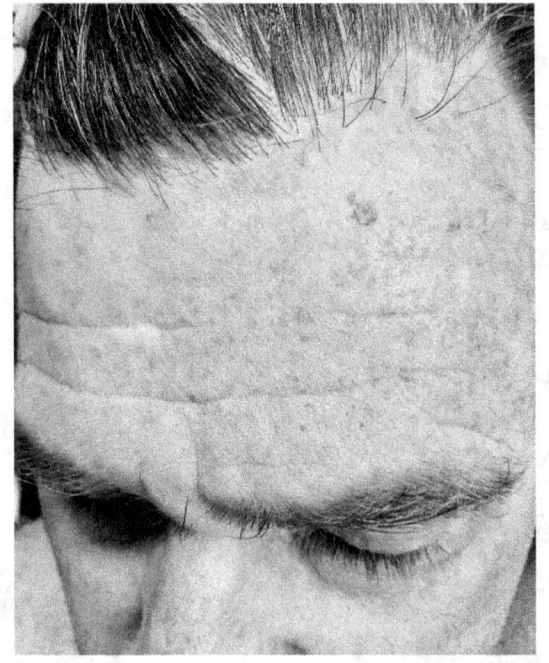

Photo: Surgery, upper forehead, to the left, that white scar was sewn by surgeons to intentionally blend in with the crease mark of my forehead – I think they did a great up!

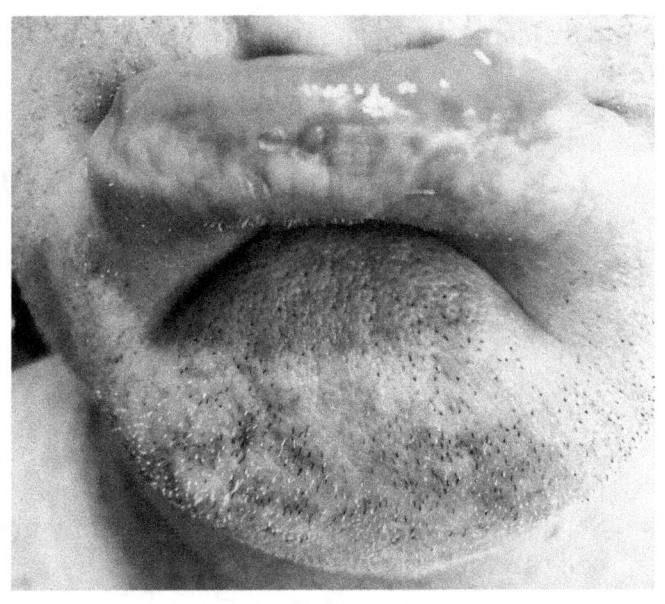

Photo: Lower face, showing lower left lip on which three Mohs surgeries have been performed from 2006 to 2018. They are highly invasive and very unattractive to look at. The Basal cells keep coming back, even when burned off periodically, so I've given up on having the big painful surgeries on this spot, since they recur. A contributing factor must be the hundreds of thousands of times I placed cigarettes on the part of my anatomy.

You cut me up:

Since 2006 over twenty Mohs surgical procedures, in Connecticut and New York City, at the preeminent cancer treatment center Memorial Sloan Kettering:

- o 5 on face
- o 3 to lower right lip
- o 7 to shoulders
- o 2 to back
- o 2 to torso
- o 3 to neck & ear
- o 2 to upper legs

- Surgeries will be ongoing due to sun damage, risk of skin cancer
- So far have had basal cell carcinoma, squamous cell carcinoma, but not melanoma

Photo: Left cheek, showing another impressive surgical job, in which a large scar with stiches was covered up as part of my smile. I was overdue to have the "inner" stitches removed and was in a dentist chair unable to make it to the dermatologist's that Friday so there would be delays. As a courtesy the understanding dentist cut and plucked out the stitches – for free! Very kind; he read the Hippocratic Oath, clearly!

Let's log that:

Diary; July 19, 1995: Dental, skin scans, Newport.

Diary; February 28, 2000: Newport, Three Lee's Wharf, following fire and sinking of the classic wooden yacht *Stiarna*; off Trinidad on February 23. Confirm with Jenna at Skin Medicine, the dermatologist in Warwick. For any prescriptions reach out to Karen at the pharmacy on Wellington Avenue down off Lower Thames Street.

Diary; November 30, 2001: Newport, Skin Medicine Center, Washington Square.

Diary; June 28, 2002: Newport: Contact skin surgery, diagnose and repair sun damage.

Diary; December 5, 2007: Appointment with Connecticut Dermatology in Norwalk.

Diary; September 5, 2008: Connecticut Dermatology gave me discounts during the financial crisis starting in September, 2008. This was particularly appreciated as it was unasked for an appreciated, my unemployment resulting therefrom as I was in the executive recruiting sector, which went from "hiring to firing."

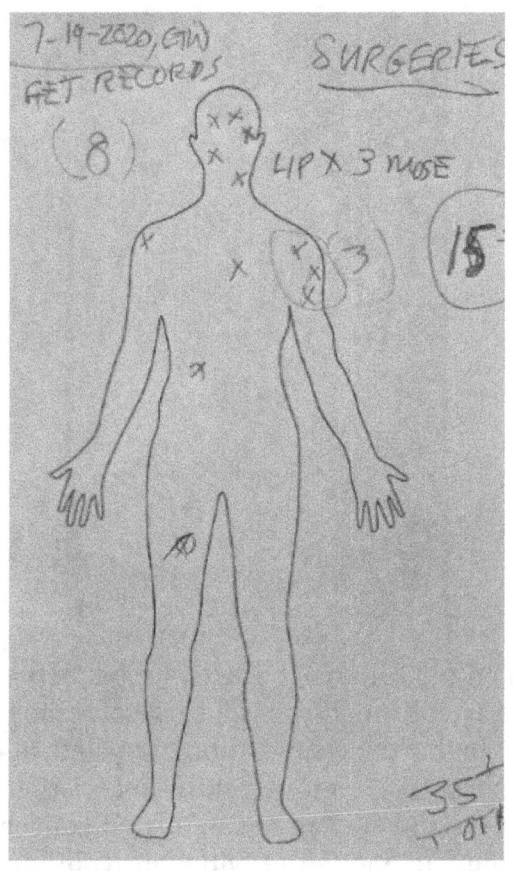

Photo: Etching of surgeries; a low estimation only, since no single doctor out of a dozen in Newport, Nassau, Singapore, New York, Westport, Boston, or Norwalk has all the records.

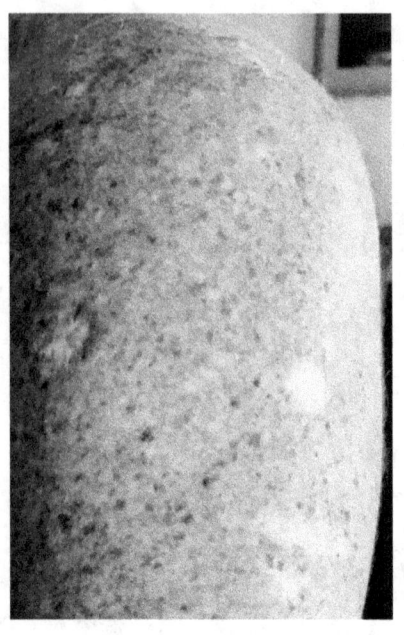

Photo: The most damaged area; upper left shoulder. From top to bottom, there is a surgical removal on top at the flat bit barely visible, then to the left, at center is another surgically removed skin cancer spot. At right, center the round spot is a scar-turned-cancerous, and the rectangular one is the wide cut from jumping off the grounded boat near Turtle Island in Singapore in 1996, which didn't heal well.

Finally an unknown scar, which appears surgically altered at bottom. This is just an image of the front of his shoulder. There are no vaccination marks or self-inflicted scars on the left side, as I smoked with my left hand and never damaged my left side.

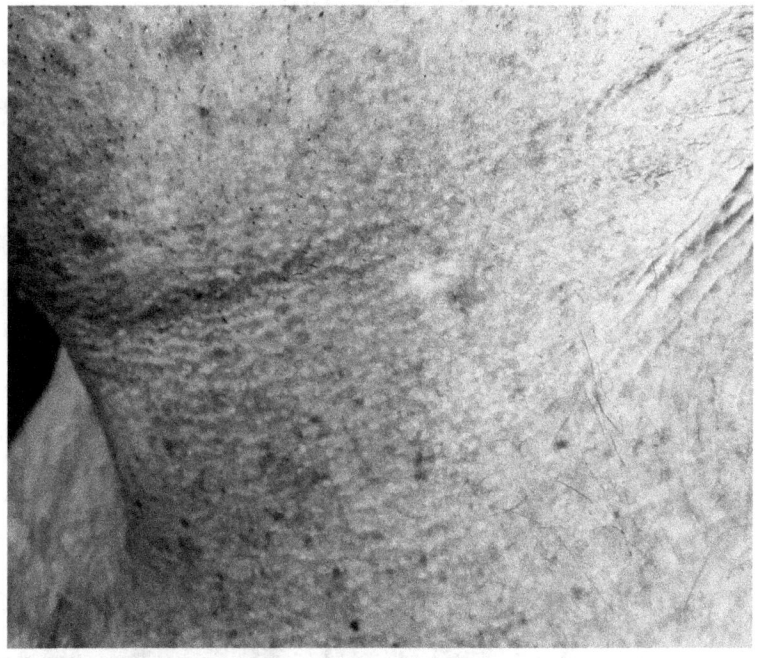

Photo: One of the many smaller surgical removals of Basal cell carcinoma removed over the years; this one on the left side of my neck.

Conclusion

My parting advice to aspiring scar-wars material?
Wear sunblock to avoid scars!
……and don't tell bulls what to do.

Footnotes:

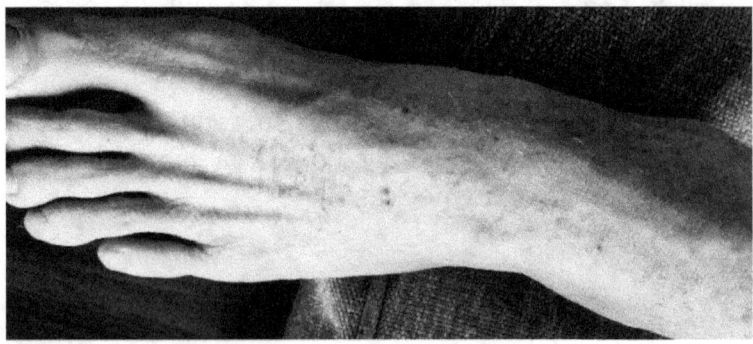

Cheeky Endnotes:

Photo: Meant to show a stark contrast between the lower back, where sun damaged caused myriad freckles, and below the customary belt line, where the sun rarely shone.

About the Author

Eric Wiberg grew up in the Bahamas and has studied in the US and EU. Though a career in shipping, salvage, tug, media, and yacht firms took him to various places, New England has been his base since boarding school in 1983. The author of roughly 30 books and nearly 1,000 articles and blog posts, Eric's strategy was to live the first 40 years as though they would be his last, and devote the rest documenting the first. He has appeared in French, Norwegian, and Spanish documentaries. His work has been used by writers for *Rolling Stone*, *Vanity Fair*, and the *Boston Globe*, and the *New York Post* called *U-Boats in New England*, a Book of the Week in December, 2019.

Eric's research led to the discovery of US, Italian, German, and Norwegian KIA in World War II, and resulted in the US Navy correcting the records for the sinking of U-84 northeast of the Bahamas, with awards made in the US Senate. Licensed as a captain since age 25 and in law a decade later, he has held jobs in Connecticut, Boston, Manhattan, the Bahamas, New Zealand, and Singapore and travelled to all continents except Antarctica.

www.ingramcontent.com/pod-product-compliance
Lightning Source LLC
Chambersburg PA
CBHW070431010526
44118CB00014B/2003